Bristol

· ·

A guide to good living

First published in Great Britain in 2010 by Alastair Sawday Publishing Limited in collaboration with the Bristol Green Capital Initiative.

Alastair Sawday Publishing Limited
The Old Farmyard
Yanley Lane
Long Ashton
Bristol BS41 9LR
www.sawdays.co.uk

Project Manager: Emily Nicholson
Managing Editor: Lyn Hemming
Editor: Emily Walmsley
Design: Open Communication Design Ltd. www.open-comms.com

Printed, foiled and bound in Great Britain by Butler Tanner and Dennis Ltd of Frome, Somerset.

This book was printed in the UK by Butler Tanner and Dennis, saving the environmental cost of long-distance transportation. The printing facility has all operations under one roof and employs mainly local people. It is certified to ISO 14001 and is aiming to achieve carbon neutrality soon. The book was printed using 100% vegetable-based inks on Ardent Offset FSC paper. Ardent Offset FSC is produced from 100% Elemental Chlorine Free (EFC) pulp that is fully recyclable. It has a Forest Stewardship Council (FSC) certification and is fully manufactured on one site by UPM Energy & Pulp in Finland, an ISO 14001 certified company. All FSC certified papers are produced by companies who support well-managed forestry schemes, which in turn actively plant and replace trees that are cut down for pulp. UPM Energy & Pulp typically plants more trees than are harvested as part of its remit.

ISBN 978-1-906136-51-2

Mixed Sources
Product group from well-managed forests and other controlled sources
www.fsc.org Cert no. SGS-COC-005091
© 1996 Forest Stewardship Council

Bristol

A guide to good living

BRISTOL
GREEN
CAPITAL
INSPIRING CHANGE

Alastair
Sawday's

Contents

Folly at Blaise Castle Estate

Foreword

by Alice Roberts

I've lived in Bristol most of my life. I think it's a place that attracts and holds on to a certain type of person—and most of the people I know and meet in the city seem to have a deep appreciation of, and respect for, the environment they live in. One of the main things I really value about Bristol as a city is its green-ness.

Literally speaking, Bristol has a wealth of green spaces, so you are always close to a place where you can feel grass under your feet instead of concrete, and look up at trees instead of buildings. I grew up climbing trees, exploring paths through the woods and generally getting very muddy in Blaise Castle Estate. But there are also green spaces right in the heart of the city that I love—precious oases in an urban environment—like Royal Fort Gardens, Castle Park and Redland Green.

Green spaces keep us in touch with nature, with the rhythm of the seasons, with the sun, wind and rain that we spend too much time hiding from. Green spaces also form venues where communities can gather: from the May Fair in Redland to the International Balloon and Kite Festivals at Ashton Court.

Bristol seems to be renowned for its green spaces. People who don't live here often remark on how lucky we are to have all this greenery on our doorsteps. But it must be good judgement on our part as well as luck, and we must be careful not to take this great asset for granted, but work to make sure that Bristol stays green for the future.

Of course, as well as all that literal greenery, Bristol has a well-deserved reputation for sustainability, environmental awareness and action. Bristol is the birthplace of Sustrans, the sustainable transport charity and originator of the national cycle network. There's a great synergy between what's good for us and what's good for the environment. Bristol may be quite hilly but that just means—as a cyclist or pedestrian—you get fitter (as I tried to remind myself while cycling up Park Street the other day). I'm looking forward to trying out some of the cycling tours in this guide.

I also love being able to stand right in the centre of Bristol and see the rural, green hills of Dundry in the distance. Every Wednesday, the country comes into the city, as local producers set up their stalls on Corn Street for the weekly Farmers Market. And once a month, on a Sunday, you can take time to enjoy the tastes of the Slow Food Market.

Bristolians are certainly not just a bunch of hippies with eco-dreams. Simple living, sustainable development and local food production are realities here, and they are making their mark on the city. This guidebook forms an ideal introduction to some of the people and places who are making and keeping Bristol green. Join the movement!

Alice Roberts is an anatomist, author and broadcaster. She has presented many BBC television programmes, including Coast *and* Digging for Britain, *and is a presenter on Radio 4's environment programme,* Costing the Earth.

Bristol Harbourside

Introduction

by Alastair Sawday

Lift a stone and you can find a world of wildlife beneath it. Get under the skin of Bristol and you will discover a vigorous, enterprising, eclectic, unorthodox and surprisingly green city. Is it our maritime and industrial history that generates this energy? Or the floating harbour, the diverse urban villages, the universities? Who knows where it comes from. What we do know is that Bristol is buzzy and happening. Graduates like to stay here; others pour in, attracted by the vibe.

The city is alive with ideas, organisations and businesses that are adding to the rich culture just as they are living from it. We have our problems— not all our ideas have been good ones—but there is a new openness about our institutions, a new willingness to embrace the challenges of the 21st century. In fact, we want to take the lead. So much so that we were the UK's only entry to the 2009 European Green Capital City competition. We didn't win, but we are now committed.

In order to win next time, we need to maintain the momentum. The Soil Association, Sustrans, the Environment Agency, the Bristol Natural History Consortium—all are adding to the chorus singing for change. So are the Zoo, St Werburghs City Farm, the Tobacco Factory and many more enterprises well known within Bristol. We have accepted the need to adapt to make ourselves less vulnerable to peak oil and climate change. The city has set itself tough carbon reduction targets and has plans to create a Bristol Energy Company, to refit thousands of buildings and to improve our food security. We have policies aplenty. If they work it will be because Bristolians in their thousands are on board. And if you skim through this book you will see that they really are.

Two crude but helpful measures of a city's open-mindedness are the number of cyclists and the number of media companies. Given its hills, Bristol has an astonishing number of keen pedallers; it is officially a Cycling City. And we have more than 1,300 media companies, from tiny to huge. Both communities are independent and feisty in their approach to life. Bristol is infected with this sort of spirit.

Cotham Hill shops

This guide is about Bristol, about what Bristolians are doing, area by area, to make their city a better and a greener place. Some are transforming their neighbourhoods through street parties and community allotment projects. Some are working hard to support their local shops and city farms, and actively and intelligently battling further supermarket incursions. Others are quietly helping their neighbours or setting up innovative green enterprises. There is even a project to measure the city's happiness—and further increase it.

If the guide is focused on green activities it is because they are now urgently necessary, and green is what Bristol has decided to become. Have a close look at the illustrated map that comes with this guide, and you will see that sustainable community projects can be found in all corners of the city. The Green Capital Momentum Group, working closely with the City Council, coordinates, encourages, articulates and nurtures green ideas and enterprise. It is very busy.

So take this book and see for yourself. It is an original and delightful guide to discovering Bristol.

Alastair Sawday has lived in Bristol for 35 years. He chairs the Green Capital Momentum Group and is a publisher and writer.

How to use this guide

> **"Things should be made as simple as possible, but not any simpler."**
>
> **Albert Einstein**

Areas

This guide is made up of eight different area sections of Bristol: South Central, South End, East Central, Central, Citywide, North End, North East and North Central. Do these areas sound familiar? Probably not. That's because this guide covers the whole expanse of Bristol, from Avonmouth to Whitchurch, and has divided the city along new lines. The idea is to break down old boundaries, to bring local communities together in new ways and to encourage both Bristolians and visitors to view the city afresh.

Each section contains information that relates to the neighbourhoods and City Council wards within that area. These can be found on the map outlines at the beginning of each chapter.

Some chapters are longer than others but the content for each follows the same pattern: introduction, tours, directory listings and case studies. The Citywide area is an exception, including just an introduction and directory listings. All places in the tours and case studies can be found in the listings so long as contact details exist for them. In some tours, locations such as parks and historic buildings may not have contact information and therefore do not appear in the directory.

Tours

There are two tours in each of the seven regional areas. These include both walking and cycling tours: some are better walked than cycled, and vice versa, and some are longer than others. The quickest can be pedalled in under an hour and the longest can be stretched out to a full day of exploration. The kinds of places the tours highlight are very much determined by the area they cover and what we found going on there. So, be prepared for some tours that are a visual treat, others that are more interactive, and others that focus on specific interests, such as food

Queen Square

or green open spaces. We do encourage you to supplement the tour directions in this guide with a Bristol A-to-Z street map or use Google maps if you'd rather (for more information about maps please read the travel information on pp. 16–17).

Bristol facts and loves

In each section there are facts about Bristol and quotes by residents about why they love the city. These have come to us from different sources: the facts are from Bristol City Council's report *Quality of Life in Bristol 2009*; the 'loves' were recorded at the Bristol Festival of Nature in June 2010 and on the website www.goodliving.org.uk. We are grateful to Bristol City Council for their permission to use the findings in their report and for the input from Bristolians about why they love this city so much.

Directory listings

Use the listings to find out about many more places than the tours and case studies can allow for. The listings cover up to 20 different place types, ranging from sustainability to built environment to food. More information about these place types can be found on pp. 12–15. The listings provide phone numbers, websites, email addresses and postal addresses to enable you to find out more about each place and to follow the interesting avenues they open up. Many listings are for projects and enterprises that invite you to become involved either by volunteering, or by using their goods and services, or by visiting them in person to learn more. The range of listings is extensive and will open your eyes to the many green and good living activities going on around the city.

Illustrated map

The Bristol Good Living Map, illustrated by Rebecca Howard, provides a descriptive view of the city as a whole. It highlights the good living activities going on in every neighbourhood, and draws attention to the many green open spaces that Bristol has to offer. Pin it on your wall and be inspired!

Clifton Suspension Bridge

Explaining place types

 ## Arts , crafts and design

A broad category that includes artisans of traditional arts and crafts as well as fine artists, graphic designers and the printing industry.

 ## Biodiversity

Places and organisations that refer to the many green open spaces in Bristol, and the groups of people who work hard to maintain and improve the biodiversity within them.

 ## Built environment

Places that provide services and advice about the built environment, such as architects and building contractors. Also places that are known for their distinctive architectural and historical features.

 ## Cafés and restaurants

Treating yourself to the occasional meal out with friends is an important part of good living. The places in this category are all run by people who are dedicated to serving good-quality, well-sourced, seasonal food.

 ## Clothing

Shops selling clothing that is either retro and second-hand, or ethical, fairtrade and organic.

Self-build eco-homes in Ashley Vale

 ## Community

Groups that share a common interest, such as sustainability, local heritage or neighbourhood well-being, within a local or citywide area.

 ## Community centres

Bristol has many new and improved centres for bringing together members of the community. The wide-ranging programmes on offer are often impressive. Some centres listed here, such as the Create Centre and the 3rd Floor, cater for certain interest groups rather than particular locations.

 ## Energy

Places that are forging ahead with developing renewable technologies, working with people to reduce their energy use, and finding ways to increase energy efficiency for all of us living and working in the city.

 ## Entertainment

You don't need to be a visitor to Bristol to nose around its local attractions. Get out there with a fresh pair of eyes and look up the places in this category to rediscover and enjoy your local treasures.

Ethical finance

Entering a new phase in world economics requires some progressive thinking by our financiers. These places all prioritise ethical finance, and some consider doing without money altogether, instead trading goods and services in kind.

 ## Family

Places that provide interest for all the family—children and adults alike. The variety within this category ensures that there is something to suit all tastes.

 ## Food

How is Bristol feeding itself? Do you know where your food comes from? The numerous places listed under this category show the enthusiasm in the city for growing and eating good, nutritious and fair food.

 ## Health and well-being

Living the good life requires a certain amount of good health. These places help to improve well-being and encourage us all to lead healthier, more holistic lives.

 ## Home

Stores that help you create a cosy nest with goods that are natural, ethical or local. Some also refurbish recycled household items, offering good value prices and reducing waste going to landfill.

 ## Information and education

A broad category taking in groups working with young people, publications that list local events, and organisations that inform a range of audiences with different interests.

 ## International development

From a Bristol base, these businesses and organisations reach out around the globe to provide advice, technical resources and, in some cases, much needed funding.

 **Sustainability**

A broad category that includes diverse organisations, businesses and enterprises concerned with the environment and sustainable development. They all work with the aim of protecting our natural resources for future generations.

 Transport

Need to get somewhere? The places and people in this category are striving to get Bristol moving—in a healthier, fairer, more efficient way.

 Volunteering

Organisations that support volunteering or are primarily set up to provide volunteering opportunities.

 Waste and recycling

When is waste not waste? When it is someone else's resource. Everything that is produced can either be reused or recycled. These listings include projects that want to make rubbish history.

Travel information

Getting around

The guide contains a number of tours that will take you on journeys of discovery across Bristol. From Avonmouth to Withywood, Clifton Village to Oldbury Court Estate, there is a wealth of places to visit and to see good living taking root. To help you find them and make full use of this guide this section provides a round-up of ways to travel around the city.

Maps

We encourage you to seek out Stanfords Map and Book Store (www.stanfords.co.uk) on Corn Street to purchase a good A-to-Z street map of Bristol. There are also many free maps and guides available from Bristol City Council, which will help you enjoy the city without a car. For journey planning, bus times, ferry rides, cycling, walking and parking information go to www.travelbristol.org.

Cycling

Cycling is taken very seriously in Bristol, as demonstrated by its status as Britain's first Cycling City. A significant investment has been made to improve infrastructure and encourage more people to cycle. The aim is to improve air quality, reduce traffic congestion and make the roads safer. The Better by Bike website (www.betterbybike.info) contains all the information you need on how to get around Bristol by bike.

Walking

If you explore the tours in this guide by foot there are complete directions given for each one. There are also a number of other routes and maps available if you wish to venture further:

- The Triangular City Walk is a long-distance walk of 18 miles that offers wonderful views of the city.
- Walk Eastside offers two mp3 audio tours that can be downloaded free of charge.
- The South Bristol Circular Walk is a long-distance city walk of approximately 23 miles.

For further information and details of how to get copies of these routes visit www.bristol.gov.uk/walking.

Bus travel

Bristol has a wide network of public transport routes. Buses are a good way to get around the city without the hassle of finding parking. For timetables, fares and a map of local bus routes visit www.bristol.gov.uk/public transport. For more information on local public transport routes you can also contact Traveline on 0871 200 2233.

Train travel

Bristol has a network of train stations across the city, which are stops on lines to Weston-super-Mare, Bristol Parkway and Severn Beach. Trains are a great way to explore the city—especially areas further out from the centre—and see it from a very different perspective. Timetables and fare information can be found at www.firstgreatwestern.co.uk or by calling National Rail Enquiries on 08457 484950.

Ferry travel

The Bristol Ferry Boat Company operates ferries daily from various locations around the harbour. Many people use these ferries to commute, but they are also a wonderful way to enjoy another view of the city. For more information call 0117 927 3416 or go to www.bristolferry.co.uk.

Driving and parking

If you do need to drive there are a number of conveniently located car parks providing easy access to the city. A map and a car park finder tool can be found at www.bristol.gov.uk/carparks.

Tourist information

To access a range of tourist information, including further transport details for journeys across Bristol, call the tourist information office on 0333 3210101 or go to http://visitbristol.co.uk.

Southville

Windmill
Hill

Bedminster

Knowle

South Central

South Central has a burgeoning community spirit that gives the area a strong, distinctive identity. The growing number of independent shops, businesses and community projects are bringing new residents in and old neighbours back together after a period of economic decline.

The change has been driven by individuals such as George Ferguson, who resurrected an old Wills building into the successful Tobacco Factory in the late 1990s. More recently, larger numbers of locals are setting up park groups, street parties and local festivals. The neighbourhoods of Ashton, Southville, Bedminster, Windmill Hill, Totterdown and Knowle are also the lucky stewards of some of Bristol's finest parks and open spaces. Just down the road is the grand and much-loved Ashton Court Estate—a local treasure.

South Central borders the city centre but the river flowing down the Cut in between makes it feel slightly removed. Crossing over the old iron footbridges or cycling over Bedminster Bridge, the pace of life slows as you enter the leafy streets of these neighbourhoods. This part of town is home to some of Bristol's most creative types, with three well-attended arts trails taking place across the year—another event that brings neighbours closer together. Once an area housing workers for the tobacco factories and other light industries, South Central is now highly sought after by young professionals. Its closeness to the city centre combined with its strong sense of local community, growing ethic of sustainability and widespread artistic scene have made this a much-prized corner of Bristol.

Windmill Hill City Farm café

Open spaces bike tour

This cycling tour crosses South Central Bristol via parks, farms and community gardens. Starting in the vast, glorious Ashton Court Estate, where deer graze around magnificent old oak trees, the tour takes you down to Greville Smyth—the oldest park in the city—and up through Ashton Gate, Southville and Bedminster to the eastern end of this area where the views get better and better (and the hills steeper!).

Windmill Hill City Farm provides a perfect halfway point for a breather, with the animal yard and gardens providing respite from the busy road outside. From here, prepare to cycle in your lowest gear up to Victoria Park, where the water maze and panoramic views of the city skyline will make you forget any aching legs. There are more amazing vistas from Perrett's Park allotments just further on, before you finally reach the peaceful haven of Arnos Vale Cemetery.

This tour takes an hour or so to cycle, if you want to raise your heart rate, but it can also make for a leisurely half-day out. Walking will take two to three hours. Just after Greville Smyth Park, North Street has many great places to stop for refreshments. The city farm also sells good food, or you could wait for a snack until Mrs Brown's Café in Victoria Park.

 Where to start

The main entrances for Ashton Court Estate are off the A369 at Kennel Lodge Road, for the mansion and centre of the estate, and at Clifton Lodge (opposite the Bridge Road junction) for the golf course and top of the estate. The Avon Cycle Way runs from Long Ashton through the estate to Clifton Lodge.

For more travel information please refer to pp.16–17.

Ashton Court Estate

Visitor Centre, Ashton Court Mansion, Long Ashton, Bristol, BS41 9JN

Acres of wild pasture and woodland on Bristol's doorstep.

Ashton Court has 850 acres of woodland and grassland and a grand mansion house designed by Humphrey Repton. Magnificent ancient oak trees and grazing deer provide the backdrop for mountain biking, golf, walking and picnics. The estate hosts major annual events such as the Balloon Fiesta and Kite Festival.

From the mansion car park cycle down Kennel Lodge Road to the junction with the A369. Turn right and at the roundabout just beyond veer left, over the pavement, onto the tarmac path. Follow the path to the left through the tunnel. Stay on the path as it wends back down to the left, away from the busy road, and through another pedestrian tunnel. Coming out of the tunnel turn left to enter Greville Smyth Park.

Friends of Greville Smyth Park (FrOGS)

The Southville Centre, Beauley Road, Southville, Bristol, BS3 1QG

Community-based group working to improve all aspects of the park.

The oldest park in Bristol, Greville Smyth is hugely popular and well known for its splendid trees, exciting children's play area and community-led activity programme. In recent years, Friends of Greville Smyth (FrOGS) have secured new play and sports facilities, hosted numerous community events and established a wildflower meadow.

Leave the park by the corner of Ashton Road and Frayne Road. Cross over onto North Street and head up the hill, past the shops and over the roundabout by the Hen and Chicken pub. Continue to the end of North Street (a 5–10 minute cycle) and at the next roundabout turn right into Cannon Street, then immediately left into East Street. Continue down East Street to the end of the semi-pedestrianised stretch, then turn right into Philip Street. Windmill Hill City Farm is two blocks down on the right.

③ Windmill Hill City Farm

Philip Street, Bedminster, Bristol, BS3 4EA

Runs social, environmental, recreational and training activities.

See case study: 'An urban farming treasure' on p. 43.

Turn right out of the farm onto Philip Street. At the end of the road turn left and then immediately right onto Windmill Close. Follow the road under the railway line. On the other side there are steps just ahead, beside the school, that lead into Victoria Park. Either push your bike up by the side of these steps or follow the path left to enter the park just after the school buildings.

④ Victoria Park Action Group

Off Windmill Close

Community association focused on preserving and improving the park.

This green, undulating park with wide-ranging views over Bristol has a water maze, children's play area, natural gym, bowling club, tennis club and skate park. The Action Group works with the City Council, police and youth workers to improve the facilities, discourage vandalism and promote use of the park by the community.

Ride over the top of Victoria Park (stopping to look back at the stunning views and enjoy the open space) and come out onto Hill Avenue at the junction with Margate Street. Head down Margate Street, straight across St John's Lane at the bottom and into Fitzgerald Road. At the end turn right into Ravenhill Road and the first left onto Sylvia Avenue. At the top of Sylvia Avenue turn left into Bayham Road to enjoy views over Perrett's Park allotments towards the city.

⑤ Perrett's Park Allotments

Off Bayham Road

Popular allotment site with a fantastic panorama of Bristol.

The stunning south-facing views of this allotment site compensate for its very steep slopes. An important social space for the community, many people have held plots here for decades and there is currently a long waiting list. For enquiries about allotment sites across the city contact the Bristol City Council Allotments office.

Coming down Bayham Road turn right into either Brecknock Road or Haverstock Road (both opposite Perrett's Park). At the end turn right into Wells Road and first left onto Cemetery Road. At the far end of Cemetery Road is an entrance into Arnos Vale Cemetery.

I ♥ Bristol because...

of the festivals celebrating the city's culture, from bikes to ballooning.

 **6 Arnos Vale Cemetery Trust**

West Lodge, Bath Road, Bristol, BS4 3EW

An organisation preserving the architecture and wildlife of this garden cemetery.

Arnos Vale Cemetery opened in 1839, inspired by the grand cemeteries of Paris and London. Saved from demolition in the 1980s by a group of concerned locals, it has recently been refurbished and now provides a rich, beautiful haven of listed monuments and natural history.

The quickest way back into the city centre is via the cemetery's main entrance on the A4 Bath Road. Turn left outside the entrance and cycle along the A4 as it leads you into town, crossing the river and passing Temple Meads Station on your right. Alternatively, head back to the Cemetery Road entrance and out onto the A37 Wells Road. Turn right and cycle downhill until the road joins the A4 heading into town.

The Create Centre

Stroll around the southside

The neighbourhoods of south central Bristol lie just 15 minutes walk from the floating harbour but have an atmosphere all of their own. This tour takes you on a circular route across the river, leaving the city centre behind, and into the homely streets of Ashton Gate, Southville and Bedminster. In the 1980s this area was falling into economic decline but today, with the renovation of the Tobacco Factory on North Street, the dynamism of the Southville Community Development Association and many other projects driven by inspired individuals, south central Bristol is buzzing again.

Starting on the banks of the river at Create—the centre for all things environmental—the tour takes you past thriving social enterprises, independent cafés with excellent coffee and fresh food, and through streets of Victorian terraces, before heading back towards the Avon New Cut. The tour ends along the banks of the Cut, where the river rises and falls with the tide, and herons can often be spotted on the banks. Walking non-stop, the tour takes just over an hour, but to enjoy the atmosphere and get a sense of these communities take your time and check out the area's weblinks for any events before you go.

⇒ Where to start

The Create Centre is located at the far west end of Cumberland Road, 30 minutes walk from the city centre. The Harbour Link 500 bus service runs there via the city centre, Broadmead and Temple Meads station at 20 minute intervals. There is also a direct ferry service from the Watershed Media Centre to the Nova Scotia landing nearby. Create is on the National Cyclepath Route 41 from Portishead. There is limited car parking.

For more travel information please refer to pp. 16–17.

The Tobacco Factory

① Create Centre

Smeaton Road, Bristol, BS1 8XN

Vibrant environmental centre hosting events, exhibitions, offices and an eco-home.

See case study: 'An environmental hub' on p. 38.

A few yards from Create cross over the river via the old iron railway bridge and head across the small park to Clift House Road, by a large red-brick warehouse. Turn left along this road and at the other end of the warehouse is a small turning left into the Riverside Garden Centre.

② Riverside Garden Centre

Clift House Road, Southville, Bristol, BS3 1RX

Cooperatively owned and run independent garden centre.

Set on the riverbank in view of the Suspension Bridge, Riverside is one of the South West's leading independent garden centres. It stocks a huge array of garden and indoor plants that are sourced, wherever possible, from local growers and suppliers. Its café is renowned for its tasty vegetarian meals and snacks.

Head back out to Clift House Road and cross over at the traffic lights into Frayne Road, which runs alongside Greville Smyth Park. Walk the length of Frayne Road and at the end cross over into North Street, just where it joins Ashton Road on a bend. Head up North Street three blocks, past Ashton Gate school, and the Tobacco Factory is a vast red-brick building, unmissable, on the corner with Raleigh Road.

③ The Tobacco Factory

Raleigh Road, Southville, Bristol, BS3 1TF

Multi-use building that includes a bar, restaurant, market and theatre.

See case study: 'Strike a light for independents' on p. 42.

If you want a diversion via the Natural Building Store (check ahead for opening times) keep walking up North Street until you reach the roundabout by the Hen and Chicken pub. Turn right into Luckwell Road and immediately left into Chessel Street. As you walk up here look back at the prime view of the Suspension Bridge. The Natural Building Store is just at the top of the hill, opposite the church.

Did you know?

There's nothing like a sense of belonging to bring the community together and 77% of respondents in Southville think they've found the secret.

④ The Natural Building Store

109-111 Chessel Street, Bedminster, Bristol, BS3 3DQ

Sells practical, sustainable, ethical products, sourced as locally as possible.

This branch of the Bristol Green Store is based in the Old Post Office in the Chessels. Its range of sustainable, ethically-traded products includes natural paints, wood finishes and removers; natural insulation; lime putty, render and plaster; glass plaster; and wood-burning stoves. Open on Saturdays 10am–4pm and by appointment.

Retrace your steps to North Street (if you took the diversion to the Natural Building Store) and cross over at the Hen and Chicken pub into Greville Road. Walk down to the junction and continue along Greville Road as it bends round to the right, up the hill and back round to the left. As the street bends right again it turns into Stackpool Road. Take the first left by an old church into Beauley Road and the Southville Centre is immediately on the right.

⑤ The Southville Centre

Beauley Road, Southville, Bristol, BS3 1QG

Runs community projects dedicated to the environment, arts and the elderly.

See case study: 'Social enterprise in the heart of the community' on p. 41.

Follow Beauley Road down to the bottom and turn left onto Coronation Road. Walk along this busy road for a few minutes until you reach the paved footbridge on your right. Cross over the river here, on the stretch known as the Avon New Cut.

⑥ Friends of the Avon New Cut (FrANC)

The Southville Centre, Beauley Road, Southville, Bristol, BS3 1QG

Local organisation promoting greater understanding of the Cut.

The Cut is a tidal waterway, rich in flora and fauna, running through Bristol. FrANC promotes greater appreciation of its history, geology, wildlife, bridges, and bank-side buildings by running guided walks and clean-up sessions and publishing a newsletter. Excavated in the early 1800s, the Cut was essential to developing Bristol's floating harbour.

Once across the river join the 'Chocolate Path' below the bridge and head west, keeping the river on your left. This cyclist and pedestrian path runs along this stretch of the New Cut all the way to the Create Centre. Once back at Create catch a bus from Cumberland Road, or a ferry from the Nova Scotia, landing back to the city centre or Temple Meads station.

Directory

 acta

Gladstone Street, Bedminster, Bristol, BS3 3AY
0117 953 2448
info@acta-bristol.com
www.acta.f2s.com

Community theatre company promoting access to the arts across Bristol.

 ## Arnos Vale Cemetery Trust

West Lodge, Bath Road, Bristol, BS4 3EW
info@arnosvale.org.uk
www.arnosvale.org.uk

An organisation preserving the architecture and wildlife of this garden cemetery.

Did you know?

We'd all like to have a shorter commute—in Bedminster only 17% of respondents are happy with the amount of local employment available.

 ## Ashton Court Estate

Visitor Centre, Ashton Court Mansion, Long Ashton, Bristol, BS41 9JN
0117 963 9174
ashton.court@bristol.gov.uk
www.bristol.gov.uk

Acres of wild pasture and woodland on Bristol's doorstep.

 ## The Beer Factory

Unit A, The Old Brewery, Durnford Street, Ashton, Bristol, BS3 2AW
0117 902 6317
www.bristolbeerfactory.co.uk

Independent brewery with a local, community focus.

 ## Bristol Fairtrade Network

Create Centre, Smeaton Road, Bristol, BS1 6XN
0117 922 4916
www.bristolfairtradenetwork.org.uk

Umbrella organisation for local volunteers and businesses
supporting fair trade.

 ## Bristol Women's Workshop

138-144, Wells Rd, Totterdown, Bristol, BS4 2AG
anne@bristolwomensworkshop.org.uk
www.bristolwomensworkshop.org.uk

Gives women experience in traditionally male skills such as woodwork
and DIY.

 ## BTCV Avon

Create Centre, Smeaton Road, Bristol, BS1 6XN
0117 929 1624
avon@btcv.org.uk
www.2.btcv.org.uk

Volunteering organisation supporting conservation initiatives in the
Avon area.

The Centre for Sustainable Energy

3 St Peters Court, Bedminster Parade, Bristol, BS3 4AQ
0117 934 1400
info@cse.org.uk
www.cse.org.uk

National charity acting to reduce non-sustainable energy consumption.

The Centre helps the public, private and voluntary sectors meet the twin challenges of rising energy costs and climate change. It gives advice and training, manages innovative energy projects and undertakes policy analysis to empower communities to develop environmentally sound and affordable energy services.

 # Climate Works Ltd

Tobacco Factory, Raleigh Road, Southville, Bristol, BS3 1TF
0117 902 0697
office@climate-works.co.uk
www.climate-works.co.uk

Sustainability and climate change consultancy.

 # Co Housing Bristol

38 Brendon Road, Windmill Hill, Bristol, BS3 4PL
0117 904 8611
www.cohousingbristol.org.uk

Cooperative seeking to build a socially, environmentally and financially sustainable neighbourhood.

 # The Community of Perrett's Park

291 Sylvia Avenue, Knowle, Bristol, BS3 5BX
thecommunityofperrettspark@blueyonder.co.uk
www.thecommunityofperrettspark.co.uk

Encourages locals to take part in caring for and improving the park.

 # Create Centre

Smeaton Road, Bristol, BS1 6XN
0117 925 0505
create@bristol.gov.uk
http://www.bristol.gov.uk

Vibrant environmental centre hosting events, exhibitions, offices and an eco-home.

See case study: 'An environmental hub' on p. 38.

FareShare South West

Unit 4a Templegate Park, Mead Rise, Bristol, BS3 4RP
0117 971 1005
info@faresharesouthwest.org.uk
www.faresharesouthwest.org.uk

Redistributes surplus produce from the food and drink industry to
disadvantaged people.

 ## Fiducia Press

10 Fairfield Road, Southville, Bristol, BS3 1LG
0117 985 2795
fiducia@blueyonder.co.uk

Not-for-profit publisher specialising in local social history.

 ## Fig 1

51 St Lukes Road, Totterdown, Bristol, BS3 4RX
0117 330 8167
enquiries@fig1.co.uk
www.fig1.co.uk

Independent gift shop promoting unusual items from small producers.

 ## Footprint Building Limited

155a South Liberty Lane, Ashton Vale, Bristol, BS3 2TL
0117 317 9571
hello@footprintbuilding.co.uk
www.footprintbuilding.co.uk

Innovative, eco-friendly company offering a premium service in
construction, property refurbishment and joinery.

 ## Forest of Avon Trust

The Estate Office, Ashton Court Estate, Bristol, BS41 9JN
0117 963 3383
jonclark@forestofavontrust.org
www.forestofavon.org.uk

Charitable organisation championing trees across the West of England.

Forest of Avon Wood Products

Bower Ashton Wood Yard, Kennel Lodge Road, Bristol, BS3 2JT
0117 966 4432
info@forestofavonproducts.co.uk
www.forestofavonproducts.co.uk

Cooperative promoting sustainable woodland projects and wood crafts in the West.

See case study: 'A feedback loop of sustainability' on p. 39.

 ## Friends of the Avon New Cut (FrANC)

The Southville Centre, Beauley Road, Southville, Bristol, BS3 1QG
0117 923 1039
info@southvillecentre.org.uk
www.franc.org.uk

Local organisation promoting greater understanding of the Cut.

 ## Friends of Callington Road Nature Reserve

16 Queens Road, Knowle, Bristol, BS4 2LT
07855 553261
http://sites.google.com/site/focrnr

Manages the nature reserve in partnership with the City Council.

 ## Friends of Greville Smyth Park (FrOGS)

The Southville Centre, Beauley Road, Southville, Bristol, BS3 1QG
0117 923 1039
info@frogs.org.uk
www.frogs.org.uk

Community-based group working to improve all aspects of the park.

 ## Green Bean Café

209 North Street, Bedminster, Bristol, BS3 1JH
0117 939 4724
glyn@the-green-bean.co.uk
www.the-green-bean.co.uk

Fairtrade, organic café—'indulgence with a conscience'.

The Green Register Map

Create Centre, Smeaton Road, Bristol, BS1 6XN
0117 377 3490
mail@greenregister.org.uk
www.greenregister.org.uk

Provides training in sustainable building practices and a register of green construction professionals.

Life Cycle UK

Create Centre, Smeaton Road, Bristol, BS1 6XN
0117 353 4580
post@lifecycleuk.org.uk
www.lifecycleuk.org.uk

Organisation that encourages and supports cycling.

Life Cycle UK equips people with the skills, knowledge and confidence to make cycling part of their everyday lives. It helps with a multitude of bike related issues, such as teaching people to cycle safely, carrying out cycle training, providing bike maintenance and setting up free cycle parking.

Linkage Walking Group

Monica Wills House, West Street, Bedminster, Bristol, BS3 3NH
0117 900 2338
joanna.yarham@bristolpct.nhs.uk
www.bristol.gov.uk

Supports the elderly through community activities and group walks.

Mark's Bread

291 North Street, Southville, Bristol, BS3 1JU
07910 979384
mark@marksbread.co.uk
www.marksbread.co.uk

Artisan breads handmade with organic flour from Gloucestershire.

See case study: 'Self-raising ambition on the high street' on p. 40.

Mrs Brown's Café

In Victoria Park
07786 275011

Serves cakes, tea, coffee and other refreshments—open April to October.

 ## National Federation of City Farms and Community Gardens

The Greenhouse, Hereford Street, Bristol, BS3 4NA
0117 923 1800
admin@farmgarden.org.uk
www.farmgarden.org.uk

Supports and promotes community-managed farms and gardens.

 ## The Natural Building Store

109-111 Chessel Street, Bedminster, Bristol, BS3 3DQ
07790 759748
http://bristolgreenstore.co.uk

Sells practical, sustainable, ethical, locally sourced products.

 ## Perrett's Park Allotments

Off Bayham Road
0117 922 3737
allotments@bristol.gov.uk
www.bristol.gov.uk

Popular allotment site with a fantastic panorama of Bristol.

 ## The Pigeon

PO Box 240, Bristol, BS10 5XG
0117 944 5512
editor@the-pigeon.com
www.the-pigeon.com

Community magazine for South Bristol.

 ## Resource Futures Map

Create Centre, Smeaton Road, Bristol, BS1 6XN
0117 930 4355
info@resourcefutures.co.uk
www.resourcefutures.co.uk

Not-for-profit consultancy advising on resource conservation.

Riverside Garden Centre

Clift House Road, Southville, Bristol, BS3 1RX
0117 966 7535
info@riversidegardencentre.com
www.riversidegardencentre.com

Cooperatively owned and run independent garden centre.

 # The Schumacher Society

Create Centre, Smeaton Road, Bristol, BS1 6XN
0117 903 1081
richard@schumacher.org.uk
www.schumacher.org.uk

Seeking practical solutions to build a sane, humane and
ecological society.

See case study: 'Pioneer environmentalists—the Schumacher story'
on p. 126.

 # South Bristol Riverscapes

Bristol Living Rivers Project, Create Centre, Smeaton Road,
Bristol, BS1 6XN
0117 922 4452
cathy.derrick@bristol.gov.uk
www.southbristolriverscapes.org.uk

Website connecting all river projects in south Bristol.

 # The Southville Centre

Beauley Road, Southville, Bristol, BS3 1QG
0117 923 1039
info@southvillecentre.org.uk
www.southvillecentre.org.uk

Runs community projects dedicated to the environment, arts and
the elderly.

See case study: 'Social enterprise in the heart of the community'
on p. 41.

Southville Deli

262 North Street, Southville, Bristol, BS3 1JA
0117 966 4507
www.southvilledeli.com

Sells a range of organic products and wholefoods.

 ## St Johns Community Association

52 St Johns Road, Bedminster, Bristol, BS3 4JJ
0117 330 6656
christopher-se1@blueyonder.co.uk
http://stjohnscommunityassociation.blogspot.com

Works to improve the environment and facilities in the neighbourhood.

 ## Sustainable Knowle

85 Somerset Road, Knowle, Bristol, BS4 2HT
0117 971 7023
http://sustainableknowle.blogspot.com

Local Transition group promoting sustainability and low carbon lifestyles.

 ## The Tobacco Factory

Raleigh Road, Southville, Bristol, BS3 1TF
0117 963 0960
building@tobaccofactory.com
www.tobaccofactory.com

A multi-use building that includes a bar, restaurant, market and theatre.

See case study: 'Strike a light for independents' on p. 42.

Transition BS3

The Green Store, 109-111 Chessel Street, Bristol, BS3 3DQ
07958 109312
josou@blueyonder.co.uk
www.transitionbs3.co.uk

Develops inspiring community responses to issues of peak oil and climate change.

The Travel Foundation

Create Centre, Smeaton Road, Bristol, BS1 6XN
0117 927 3049
admin@thetravelfoundation.org.uk
www.thetravelfoundation.org.uk

Charity promoting sustainability in the travel and tourism industry.

A Bristol-based charity with a global goal, the Travel Foundation helps travel companies manage tourism more responsibly. It works to protect the environment in destination countries while improving the well-being of local communities. Projects range from tree planting to supporting local supply chains to training guides to protect coral reefs.

 ## Victoria Park Action Group

Off Windmill Close
0117 922 2057
www.vpag.org.uk

Community association focused on preserving and improving the park.

 ## Voscur

Create Centre, Smeaton Road, Bristol, BS1 6XN
0117 909 9949
info@voscur.org
www.voscur.org

Development agency for Bristol's voluntary, community and social enterprise sector.

 ## Windmill Hill City Farm

Philip Street, Bedminster, Bristol, BS3 4EA
0117 963 3252
info@windmillhillcityfarm.org.uk
www.windmillhillcityfarm.org.uk

Runs social, environmental, recreational and training activities.

See case study: 'An urban farming treasure' on p. 43.

Create Centre

An environmental hub

The Create Centre is a hub of organisations working in sustainability and the voluntary sector. Housed in a striking old tobacco warehouse on the edge of the river, it is home to a host of groups and small businesses such as Resource Futures, The Green Register, Life Cycle, City Car Club, The Travel Foundation and Voscur, alongside Bristol City Council's sustainability teams. The Centre is also well known as an eco-friendly venue for meetings and conferences.

Council-owned, Create plays a dual role as an office space for green businesses and organisations, and as a visitor centre with wide-ranging resources, exhibits and public events about sustainability. It has an eco-reference library, changing exhibitions, an art gallery and a café. Next door is the Ecohome, built in 1997 by architects Bruges Tozer. This low-impact demonstration house is full of practical ideas for greener living, and also has a lovely garden where volunteers grow organic fruit, veg and flowers. The Create events programme includes family activity days, talks, workshops and adult learning courses.

Right from the start Create aimed to demonstrate sustainability in action. The 1994 refurbishment included pioneering eco-friendly features such as rainwater collection for flushing toilets, a computer-controlled energy management system and extensive recycling facilities. Further attempts to reduce its environmental impact will include solar water heating, shortly to be installed in the kitchen, and the possibility of microgeneration energy options.

The Centre fosters an environment that encourages partnership-building, provides a conducive space for formal and informal learning, and brings people together to develop new ideas. Exhibitions and events reflect this ethos. The recent exhibition on peak oil, for example, focused on the positive aspects of reducing our oil dependency and highlighted the grassroots activities of communities across the city. Transition groups helped organise a Saturday fun day to celebrate these achievements and encourage others to get involved. Sustainable action requires working together, and Create is a hub for such activities.

Forest of Avon Wood Products

A feedback loop of sustainability

Jim O'Shaughnessy is a founding member of Forest of Avon Wood Products, a dynamic marketing cooperative of sole traders, woodland owners and woodland enterprises in the West of England/Greater Bristol region. Members of the cooperative run activities, commercial and otherwise, that support the development and sustainable use of woodlands. The idea grew out of Jim's work with the Forest of Avon Partnership, where he noticed that many local woodlands remained unmanaged and woodland owners had difficulty in selling timber. He also knew that many local craftspeople could not find a local source of timber, and could not sell their products. He realised there was a demand for a local timber supply chain and that this was an ideal opportunity for creating a new cooperative—one bringing together woodland owners and craftspeople to support sustainable woodland management.

Jim's interest in nature and trees began as a teenager when he spent his free time cycling around the countryside to escape from Slough. On these rides he had many 'timeless' moments when he felt a powerful connection to nature. These experiences made him question the competitiveness of the world he was growing up in and he became deeply committed to conservation. By the time he was 16 he had discovered the idea of cooperatives and saw this as an alternative to the mainstream culture that was eroding the environment. His interest in sustainability developed when he began to realise that environmental issues have to be considered alongside social and economic needs.

Jim has been instrumental in developing the Green Arts Network Co-operative, which brings artists in at the early, creative stage of sustainability projects. He is also involved in many community initiatives, such as the Best of Bedminster Show, a celebration of local food and low carbon projects and activities. Through all these projects he has created a work–life balance that reflects his personal value system and his love of community and nature. Currently he is working with performance artists known as the Desperate Men and with the Create Centre to design a giant eco-version of Monopoly that will be used at festivals.

Mark's Bread

Self-raising ambition on the high street

Mark's Bread is a small, artisan bread-making business in North Street, just down the road from the Tobacco Factory. It's an inspiring example of someone with a dream of living a more sustainable existence, including what he does for a living. The flours used at Mark's Bread are all locally sourced and organic; the bread is made by hand using traditional methods and natural yeasts, and it is delivered by bicycle. The bakery also has a steady stream of customers through the door buying loaves still warm from the oven.

Mark Newman had been wanting a career change for some time, but it wasn't until his wife gave him a 50th birthday present of a two-day course in continental bread making that he had the idea of opening a bakery. 'I've always been interested in food but I've spent most of my working life as a computer programmer,' he says. 'When our two boys grew up and left home a few years ago, I had more scope to branch out. You only have one life, so I finally decided to quit and go for it.' This was back in 2007. He spent the next two years researching the idea and finally set up the bakery in November 2009. 'I'm following my passion. I believe if you have enthusiasm for your work then you will succeed. I had some savings and used these to buy second-hand equipment on a shoestring.'

Before long Mark had to employ assistants to keep up with demand for his bread, and he now has three full-time and three part-time staff. 'We have a great team of passionate and committed individuals. The work is hard and the hours are long, but we try to keep it fun and create a warm and welcoming environment for our customers They can see the bread being made, smell it being baked, and take it hot from the shelves.'

The Southville Centre

Social enterprise in the heart of the community

The Southville Centre is a business owned by and run for the local community. It inhabits a beautiful Victorian building in the heart of Southville that used to be home to the local secondary school, which was moved in the 1980s. Around the same time the Imperial Tobacco factory on North Street closed, impacting hugely on the local economy and community. This downturn heralded the establishing of the Southville Centre. Supported by Bristol City Council, which leased the old school at a low rate, a group of locals set up the Southville Community Development Association in 1991.

Since then, the Centre has thrived and provided the inspiration and support for numerous other community projects. Many of these have become independent yet remain linked, reinforcing the idea that collaboration is essential to creating a healthy local community. Rather than relying on external funding, the Centre sells services required in the local area back to members of the community. This ensures its financial sustainability and wealth creation—wealth being defined here as environmental and social as well as economic. 'It's this financial sustainability that allows us to support local community initiatives and provide employment for around 36 local people,' says Director Anne Malindine, who led the move to make the Centre a social enterprise.

The Centre has a café and catering facility selling largely fairtrade, locally sourced and organic ingredients. There is a nursery, holiday and after- school club, wedding license, room hire and conference facilities, which received the Gold Award from the Green Tourist Scheme. According to Anne Malindine, the key to making this forward-thinking community centre such a success has been 'to take time to build quality relationships and develop a professional infrastructure'.

The Tobacco Factory

Strike a light for independents

The Tobacco Factory was saved from demolition in 1995 by architect George Ferguson. His desire to keep the building and create something for the community has become a model of sustainable urban regeneration. Now a major landmark on North Street, it houses the Café Bar, Teohs Oriental Bistro, a creative industry workspace, live/work loft apartments, a Sunday market and one of the most exciting small theatre venues in the country.

The theatre became a full-time professional organisation in 2001 and is now a charitable trust and a Key Arts Provider of Bristol City Council. The Café Bar opened the same year and initiated the 'Strike a Light for Independents' campaign against the domination of chain bars and retail outlets. The campaign encourages the use of local shops and businesses to ensure the survival of the local community. This ethos is continued in the live/work loft apartments where space is only let to independent businesses and organisations.

The Tobacco Factory is an excellent example of how a relatively small investment can have a major effect on an area. Before the redevelopment the neighbourhood around North Street was depressed and had a high rate of vandalism and crime. The Tobacco Factory was a regeneration experiment that drew new people to the area through the social and economic activity it created, and brought the high street back to life. It sits in the heart of the community and has become a major employment hub for creative enterprises.

The Tobacco Factory is on a journey towards self-sufficiency and aims to become as close to carbon neutral as possible. Plans for the future include fixing photovoltaics on the roof, growing food in the courtyard garden, sourcing more local produce for the café and introducing meat-free Mondays. Through the Tobacco Factory George Ferguson has encouraged the spirit and energy of individuals to help the local community thrive. Its extraordinary success should be an inspiration to others to take the initiative and start something new.

Windmill Hill City Farm

An urban farming treasure

Windmill Hill City Farm is located just outside Bristol city centre, tucked away between Bedminster Parade and an industrial estate. The project was set up in 1976 by local residents who adopted a piece of derelict land. They developed it to meet the needs of local people through a range of social, environmental, recreational and economic activities. As well as the farmyard and gardening plots, its facilities include a computer centre, training rooms, play areas and a crèche.

A day visit gives you time to explore the rambling gardens and meet the healthy, well-nourished animals. The shop and café offer masses of ethical produce and delicious, freshly prepared dishes often made from ingredients produced on the farm itself. Kids can enjoy the adventure playground (recommended for ages 8–14). The farm also runs well-attended courses on farming, sustainability and crafts, which include horticulture, permaculture, embroidery, stained glass, cheese making and how to build an earth oven. Some of these are run in connection with the Workers Education Association and the Low Impact Living Initiative.

The farm is a charity run by 30 paid staff and a band of committed volunteers. It's a wonderful place for people of all ages to learn about farming, food and what it takes to develop a sustainable community. It hasn't always been an easy ride—financially things have been tough—and it's only through the generosity and dedication of staff and supporters that Bristol is lucky enough still to have this haven. The farm is highly recommended for a visit or, better still, for getting involved and becoming part of this precious city resource

Bishopsworth

Filwood

Brislington
East

Hartcliffe

Hengrove

Brislington
West

Stockwood

Whitchurch
Park

South End

The hills of Dundry rise up above the neighbourhoods of Bishopsworth, Withywood and Hartcliffe on the southern edge of Bristol. Countryside and city merge together here, with the pastimes of many residents expressing this rural–urban link. There's horse riding, community vegetable patches and numerous local conservation groups. Several estates in this area, such as Knowle West, have been settled both by those moving out of inner city Bristol and those moving in from villages in the countryside around.

Different water sources also define this area. The River Avon flows along the eastern edge of Brislington, while streams from springs on Dundry and Knowle Hill—once the only clean source of water this side of town—run down through these southern neighbourhoods. In St Anne's Wood you can still find a mediaeval well, once visited by royalty to obtain fertility rights. There are many open spaces to be explored here, with local groups working with the council to maintain and improve them.

Some parts of South End have had mixed coverage over the years, but today new projects from grassroots organisations, community centres and neighbourhood partnerships are opening up opportunities and instilling a greater sense of pride. A new cycle path from Hartcliffe into the centre of town and a better public transport service is helping to plug the outlying areas into the rest of the city. In Brislington, Knowle and St Annes, new shops, cafés, businesses and services, such as Paintworks on the Bath Road, are providing a local focus for south Bristol life.

Graffitti art in Knowle West

Paths of local knowledge

This tour is inspired by two Green Maps created by south Bristol residents, highlighting the rural nooks that exist within this built environment. One covers the Knowle West area and the other Hartcliffe and Withywood. Contact the Knowle West Media Centre and CSV Environment respectively (see the directory) for more information.

The tour starts along the Malago Greenway, a well-protected pathway linking Bedminster to the neighbourhoods further south. Walking through Manor Woods you come out near Bishopsworth Manor, a majestic Regency home that can be viewed from the road. Passing by the CSV Environment offices the tour heads southwards, through Withywood and Hartcliffe and up the hill to Dundry Spring. Artwork marks the source of the Malago River, with far-reaching views back north over Bristol. Heading back down, you re-enter the suburbs via another of the city's resourceful neighbourhood farms and community gardens.

From here, the tour heads towards the iconic Knowle West Media Centre, which has helped transform this once-deprived neighbourhood. Nearby is the shop for re:store, a good place for restored furniture that trains young people and the unemployed. A little further on, the Park Centre has a café if you need to stop for a break. Check out the Buried Treasure garden centre while you're here if staff are available. The tour ends at another spring: one that supplied fresh water to St Mary Redcliffe church in town for many hundreds of years. This tour is best done by bicycle, taking a couple of hours at a moderate pace, with occasional stops. If you walk you need to allow at least half a day and make the most of it with a picnic and supplies as places to stop for refreshments are few along the way.

⇒ Where to start

This tour starts at a point on the Malago Greenway route by Hartcliffe Way, just behind the Shell garage. From here you enter Manor Woods. There is limited car parking in this area and as the tour finishes at a different point it is easier to cycle or take the bus to the start and from the end.

For more travel information please refer to pp. 16–17.

1 Malago Valley Conservation Group

Meetings held at: St Peters Rooms near St Peters Church

Voluntary group working on local conservation issues.

The main section of the Malago Greenway runs from Bedminster to Bishopsworth and is maintained by the Malago Valley Conservation Group. This mostly off-road path is bordered at various intervals by green open spaces, play areas and even a wildlife garden converted from a derelict coal yard.

From this part of the Malago Greenway you will come out onto St Peter's Rise. Turn right at the end onto Bishopsworth Road and the manor house is a short distance up the road on the other side.

2 Bishopsworth Manor

Bishopsworth Manor, Bishopsworth Road, Bristol, BS13

Wonderful example of a Regency manor house with a formal garden.

A Grade II-listed building dating back to 1720, this beautiful manor house was restored in the 1980s by late owner Denis Bristow. It also has a formal garden that has recently been landscaped and planted. It is not open to the public but has links to the Avon Gardens Trust.

Follow Bishopsworth Road as it turns into Queen's Road. Follow this road until you reach the turning with King George's Road. You will find the CSV Environment offices here (to find out more about volunteering with this organisation call ahead).

I ♥ Bristol because...

of the cafés by the water and the houseboats.

 **3** **CSV Environment**

St David's Centre, Queen's Road, Bishopsworth, Bristol, BS13 8LF

Organisation offering volunteering opportunities on community projects.

CSV is the UK's leading charity providing volunteering and training opportunities. In Bristol the CSV Environment staff in Bishopsworth provide local people with the opportunity to build their self-esteem through voluntary environmental work and help people to set up their own projects.

This next section of the tour takes in the residential areas of Bishopsworth and Withywood and the lower slopes of Dundry Hill. From Queen's Road head up the hill until you reach Cobham Drive on your left. Go along here and turn right into Newland Road. Follow this road almost to the end and take a right into Kencot Walk to access Dundry Hill. Once on this path continue behind the housing until you reach an entrance into Aldwick Avenue. Turn right on the path and head uphill to Dundry Spring.

4 **Dundry Spring**

Off Aldwick Avenue

Source of the Malago River.

The Malago River originates from springs that issue through the limestone at Dundry Hill before heading down into Bristol's city centre. Artwork marks the site of one of the sources, now maintained by the Malago Valley Conservation Group. Dundry Hill has splendid views of south Bristol and Chew Valley.

Retrace your steps back to the entrance to Aldwick Avenue. Follow this road until you reach Bishport Avenue. Turn right here and continue to a roundabout. Turn right into Lampton Avenue and go along to the end to find Hartcliffe Community Farm.

⑤ Hartcliffe Community Farm

Hartcliffe Community Farm, Lampton Avenue, Bristol, BS13 0QH

Thirty-acre farm run by a team of 60 local volunteers.

This community farm was set up in 1930 on the northern slopes of Dundry Hill. It also provides community development through social, educational and recreational activities.

Lampton Gardens are just back down the road a few metres on the other side of Lampton Avenue.

⑥ Lampton Gardens

Lampton Gardens, off Lampton Avenue, Hartcliffe, Bristol, BS13

A green space cultivated and cared for by the community.

A CSV Environment project, this small community garden in Hartcliffe provides opportunities for volunteers to learn a wide range of horticultural skills, to meet new people and enjoy an active lifestyle.

Go back to the end of Lampton Avenue and cross straight over the roundabout into The Groves. From here follow a path through a small park and then cross Hareclive Road to access Pigeonhouse Stream Park.

⑦ Pigeonhouse Stream Park

Off Hawkfield Road, Hartcliffe, Bristol, BS13

Park route following a stream from Hartcliffe towards Hengrove.

The Pigeonhouse Stream is a tributary of the Malago River and is similarly vital for draining the slopes of Dundry Hill. The stream and surrounding park are wildlife havens for many species, in particular kingfishers. The Malago Valley Conservation Group provides care and maintenance for the area.

Carry on through this park to come out onto Whitchurch Lane. Go over the grassy area straight ahead and follow a path by the side of Hengrove Way towards a roundabout. Cross over at the new pedestrian crossings and go a short distance on Hengrove Way following signs for Bath. Take a left onto a path that takes you into Inns Court. Once in Inns Court Drive turn right and follow the road until the junction with Creswicke Road. Turn right onto Creswicke then left onto Carisbrooke Road. Follow this to the junction with St Whytes Road. Turn left at the end and then right onto Leinster Avenue. The Knowle West Media Centre can be found a few metres further along on the left-hand side.

⑧ Knowle West Media Centre

Leinster Avenue, Knowle West, Bristol, BS4 1NL

Co-creates projects with local residents to develop their potential.

See case study: 'Supporting grassroots creativity' on p. 70.

From the Media Centre head down Leinster Avenue, past a rank of shops, and turn right onto Broadbury Road. Follow this road until you get to Barnstaple Road. Take a left here and carry on to Filwood Broadway. The re:store shop will be across the green in front of you.

I ♥ Bristol because...
it feels like a place where you can just be.

⑨ re:store

17 Filwood Broadway, Knowle West, Bristol, BS4 1JL

Repairs and revamps old furniture for sale in the shop and online.

re:store is part of the charity re:work, which provides young people and those looking to return to employment with skills and opportunities. At re:store a team of young people excluded from school restore donated furniture under the guidance of an experienced woodworker. Other re:work projects include re:build and re:grow.

Head back to Barnstaple Road and cross over to Marwood Road. At the end turn right onto Connaught Road and cross over Illminster Avenue and Tavistock Walk to reach Tavistock Road. Turn right onto Daventry Road and continue along here until you see the entrance to The Park Centre on the right.

10 The Park Centre

The Park Centre, Daventry Road, Knowle, Bristol, BS4 1DQ

Hub of community activity with business, training and leisure facilities.

The Park is at the heart of the Knowle community and encompasses a wide range of facilities. On its 15-acre site it has an IT suite, conference centre, practical activity rooms, office space, sports centre and café.

Go back onto Daventry Road. Cross over and walk to the right of St Barnabas Church to access the Northern Slopes. Go over the first field, gradually getting lower on the slope, until you reach a small wooded area. After this the path splits, take the right path up the slopes again towards some more housing. As you near the top of this slope you'll see the springhead covered just before an exit onto Stockwood Crescent.

11 Pipeline Spring

Off Daventry Road, Knowle West, Bristol, BS4

Ancient route carrying water down to St Mary Redcliffe church.

In 1190 a pipeline was laid to transport water from a spring in Knowle Hill to St Mary Redcliffe church, providing the only supply of clean water for this area. Each autumn the 'walk of the pipe', an ancient Bristolian custom, takes place to protect the rights of Redcliffe parish to the water.

From the pipeline spring you could follow the pipeline all the way to the church. Alternatively, you can retrace your steps down the hill and then take the opposite path out onto Wedmore Vale. Or you can exit the slopes onto Stockwood Cresent to catch a bus. If you are on your bicycle you will be close enough to St John's Lane in Bedminster to follow main routes back into town.

Slow southern amble

This tour combines parks, nature reserves and riverbanks with some of the best cafés and bars in south Bristol. There are plenty of places for picnics if the weather's fine, or for lunch, tea, coffee or a drink if you need reviving on a grey day! The tour starts at the most southern point, in Victory Park, which is an open space well used by local residents and on the City Council's list for a makeover. From here the tour heads down to the River Avon and into the Eastwood Farm Nature Reserve, a beautiful area to explore, and well cared for by the City Council and the Friends of Eastwood Farm. Following the river around the bend you come to the tour's first great eating spot, hidden between water and woodland— Beeses Bar and Tea Gardens. If you time it right, there may be live music as you enjoy a local ale, a cream tea or an excellent dish of the locally sourced produce.

Following the river a little further, the tour wends its way through St Annes, where the small woodland and well offer another unexpected wild corner in the heart of a residential zone. Descending the hill from St Anne's Park you come to Brislington's coolest hang-out, the T Cup café bar. Hopefully you will be ready for more refreshment by now, as T Cup sells the best hot chocolate for miles around. From here, the last stretch of the tour is along Bath Road to Bristol's creative quarter at the Paintworks. This old industrial site has been transformed into a stylish live/work environment that includes offices, artist studios and flats alongside a bar, café, events space and television studios. The Tube Diner is your destination here, and it is unmissable: two chrome Airstream trailers parked in the heart of the quarter, run by the indefatigable Angie.

This tour is best walked and will take around two and a half hours. If you stop for a delicious cream tea as suggested, or you want to lounge by the river, leave yourself a good half-day to enjoy it. If you do decide to cycle be aware that it is not bike-friendly in places with park entrances, exits and steep paths.

 Where to start

*To reach Victory Park follow the A4 Bath Road out of town. Where it
becomes Brislington Hill turn left into School Road, then right into Church
Hill. At the end there is an entrance to Victory Park via the cemetery. There
is limited car parking here and as this tour finishes in a different location it
it is best to walk, cycle or catch a bus to the start and from the finish.*

For more travel information please refer to pp. 16–17.

 Victory Park

School Road, Brislington, Bristol, BS4

A large neighbourhood park with a semi-rural feel.

Set on the slopes of Brislington, surrounded by mature trees and
hedgerows, this is one of the larger parks of south Bristol. It is often
used by local sports teams and has several lookout points and a
children's play area.

*Exit the park on Bonville Road and follow it until you reach a right of way
that takes you through to Belroyal Avenue and onto Wyndham Crescent.
On this road you will find a pedestrian access for Eastwood Farm
Nature Reserve.*

 Friends of Eastwood Farm

Entrance: Whitmore Avenue, Bristol, BS4 4TH

Group that helps look after the riverside nature reserve.

Nestling on the banks of the River Avon, Eastwood Farm was used for
landfill until the 1970s. After extensive improvement, the area is now a
haven for many species of wildlife, including kingfishers, buzzards and
herons. The Friends group organises public events and ensures the area
is well-maintained for the community.

After entering the reserve you walk along the edge of a private property and down a trail that takes you to the river bank. Follow this trail along the river until you come to the entrance of Beeses Bar and Tea Gardens.

③ Beeses Bar and Tea Gardens

Conham Ferry (off Wyndham Crescent), Bristol, BS4 4SX

Fully licensed pub, restaurant and river ferry on the banks of the Avon.

See case study: 'Buzzing away on the river' on p. 66.

Walk up the hill from Beeses to come back onto Wyndham Cresent. At the junction with Eastwood Road take a right and follow this road and then Birchwood Road until it turns into Guildford Road. Take a left here into Litchfield Road. After about 12 houses on the left take a left path to access St Anne's Wood and Well. Follow the path though the woods to find the well inside.

④ St Anne's Wood and Well

Entrance: St Anne's Park Road, Brislington, Bristol, BS4

A steep, densely wooded valley with a mediaeval well.

An important historical site and wildlife haven, the area is named after the mediaeval church that previously stood here. Henry VII visited St Annes after winning the Wars of the Roses and the site is still significant for both Christians and pagans as the destination of a mediaeval pilgrimage route.

From St Anne's Well follow the path further through the wood to come out on Newbridge Road. Cross this road to access St Anne's Park.

⑤ St Anne's Park

Entrance: St Anne's Park Road, Brislington, Bristol, BS4

A popular, formally laid-out park leading to woodland and meadows.

St Anne's Park is a vital green space for residents in the Brislington area, with a well-used play zone and an active bowls club. Nearby Nightingale Valley is a mix of woodland and water meadows—an important wildlife resource well-maintained by the Friends of Nightingale Valley group.

Go back to Newbridge Road and turn right to come into Wick Road. Turn right into Colin Road and then left into Sandholme Road. Left again into Sandbach Road and cross over Upper Sandhurst Road to turn down into Sandringham Road. This arrives on Sandy Park Road where T Cup can be found to your right.

6 T Cup

53-55 Sandy Park Road, Bristol, BS4 3PH

Relaxed café with top-quality hot drinks and a tantalising menu.

Large sofas, internet access, toys for the kids: this is a cool and comfortable café for hanging out, doing some work, or enjoying a tasty meal. The teas are all sustainably sourced and the coffees organic and fairtrade. Be sure to have a taste of the 'Pimped up hot chocolate'.

Walk down Sandy Park Road to the Bath Road. Heading in the direction of town, cross a couple of sets of traffic lights and walk along until you come to the main entrance for the Paintworks on your right. Go through this entrance and you'll find the Tube Diner straight ahead of you in the shiny Airstream trailers.

I ♥ Bristol because...
my family live in Bristol.

7 The Tube Diner

Paintworks, Bath Road, Bristol, BS4 3EH

Sells fresh sandwiches, drinks and snacks out of an Airstream trailer.

See case study: 'Angie's story' on p. 71.

From the Paintworks you can easily catch a bus to anywhere in town from the Bath Road. To cycle or walk into the city centre will take 15 and 35 minutes respectively.

Bocabar, Paintworks

Directory

 ### Arno's Park Action Group

C/o Bristol City Parks, Wicklea Youth and Community Centre Road,
281 Wick Bristol, BS4 4HR
0117 922 3719
info@arnospark.org.uk
www.arnospark.org.uk

Works to improve this splendid green space for everyone's benefit.

 ### Ashton Vale Heritage Group

**Meetings held at: Ashton Vale Community Centre, Risdale Road,
Bristol, BS3 2QY**
07972 558117
mail@ashtonvaleheritage.co.uk
www.ashtonvaleheritage.co.uk

Preserves the heritage of Ashton Vale and protects threatened
green fields.

 ### Beeses Bar and Tea Gardens

Conham Ferry (off Wyndham Crescent), Bristol, BS4 4SX
0117 977 7412
info@beeses.co.uk
www.beeses.co.uk

Fully licensed pub, restaurant and river ferry on the banks of the Avon.

See case study: 'Buzzing away on the river' on p. 66.

 ### Bishopsworth Manor

Bishopsworth Manor, Bishopsworth Road, Bristol, BS13
www.avongardenstrust.org.uk

Wonderful example of a Regency manor house with a formal garden.

Bishopsworth Manor

 Bocabar

Unit 3.1 Paintworks, Arnos Vale, Bristol, BS4 3EH
0117 972 8838
bocabarbookings@btconnect.com
www.bocabar.co.uk

Lively bar in the media quarter serving local, seasonal food.

 Brislington Community Partnership

Wicklea Youth and Community Centre, 281 Wick Road,
Bristol, BS4 4HR
info@brislington.org
www.brislington.org

Neighbourhood partnership supporting projects for and by local residents.

See case study: 'Neighbourhood engagement—archaeology to skate parks' on p. 67.

 Brislington Conservation and History Society

Meetings held at: St Cuthberts Church, 35 Wick Crescent,
Bristol, BS4 4HG
0117 977 8108
bchs88@hotmail.com

Researches and discusses local history and preserves the
local environment.

Buried Treasure Ltd

The Park, Daventry Road, Knowle West, Bristol, BS4 1DQ
07810 474558
buriedtreasure2001@hotmail.com
www.buriedtreasuregarden.co.uk

Community social enterprise offering gardening services and horticultural training.

See case study: 'Greening the city' on p. 68.

The Carbon Makeover

Knowle West Media Centre, Leinster Avenue, Knowle West,
Bristol, BS4 1NL
0117 353 4604
misty@kwmc.org.uk
www.carbonmakeover.org.uk

Community project to reduce carbon emissions in our everyday lives.

CSV Environment

St David's Centre, Queen's Road, Bishopsworth, Bristol, BS13 8LF
0117 935 9710
bristol@csvenvironment.org.uk
www.csv.org.uk

Organisation offering volunteering opportunities on community projects.

Dundry Spring

Off Aldwick Avenue
www.mvcg.org.uk

The source of the Malago River.

Edible Landscapes Movement

Knowle West Media Centre, Leinster Avenue, Knowle West,
Bristol, BS4 1NL
0117 903 0444
misty@kwmc.org.uk
www.knowlewest.co.uk/projects/elm

Combined gardening and media project growing food in disused open spaces.

Filwood, Knowle and Windmill Hill Neighbourhood Partnership

37 Filwood Broadway, Bristol, BS4 1JL
0117 908 4350
neighbourhood.partnerships@bristol.gov.uk
http://bristolpartnership.org

One of five neighbourhood partnerships in south Bristol.

Friends of Eastwood Farm

Entrance: Whitmore Avenue, Bristol, BS4 4TH
0117 922 3719
friends@eastwoodfarm.org.uk
www.eastwoodfarm.org.uk

Group that helps look after the riverside nature reserve.

Friends of Nightingale Valley

Hill Lawn, Wick Road, Brislington, Bristol, BS4 4PH
cg007g1770@blueyonder.co.uk
www.brislington.org/fon/fon.html

Local group providing information about this well-hidden wildlife haven.

Friends of Stockwood Open Spaces

C/o Pete Goodwin, 11 Lanesborough Rise, Stockwood,
Bristol, BS14 8AJ
01275 543280
fosos.sec@gmail.com
www.flowershill.pwp.blueyonder.co.uk/fososintro.htm

Young group protecting local green spaces for people and wildlife.

Grassroots Urban Horse and Pony Club

The Park Centre, Daventry Road, Knowle, Bristol, BS4 1DQ
0117 903 9770
traceypool@blueyonder.co.uk
www.GrassrootsUHPC.co.uk

Promotes the use of horses for low carbon community development.

Green Footprints

The Park, Daventry Road, Knowle West, Bristol, BS4 1DQ
07810 474558
buriedtreasure2001@hotmail.com
www.green-footprints.org.uk

Grassroots enterprise growing and selling vegetable seedlings.

 ## Green Medicine

Knowle West Media Centre, Leinster Avenue, Knowle West,
Bristol, BS4 1NL
07980 530715
akilahnuru@hotmail.co.uk
www.green-medicine.org.uk

Local organisation sharing knowledge about the healing power of plants.

 ## Greenteeprints Ltd

14 Chapel Way, St Annes, Bristol, BS4 4EU
0800 612 8942
us@greenteeprints.co.uk
www.greenteeprints.co.uk

Ethical and environmentally safe t-shirt and hoody printing.

Greenteeprints also works with local artists to produce a range of unique T-shirt designs. The Mild West Heroes range can be found in the South Arcade at St Nicholas Market and at www.mildwestheroes.co.uk.

 ## Hartcliffe and Withywood Community Partnership

@Symes Resource Centre, Peterson Avenue, Hartcliffe,
Bristol, BS13 0BE
0117 903 8044
info@hwcp.org.uk
www.hwcp.org.uk

Supports local projects to create a safe, healthy, inclusive community.

 ## Hartcliffe Community Farm

Hartcliffe Community Farm, Lampton Avenue, Bristol, BS13 0HQ
0117 978 2014

Thirty-acre farm run by a team of 60 local volunteers.

Hartcliffe Food Cooperative

Unit 4 The Gatehouse Centre, Hareclive Road, Hartcliffe,
Bristol, BS13 9JN
0117 964 7228
rhian.evans@hheag.org.uk
www.hheag.org.uk

Sells organic wholefoods, fairtrade goods and local produce.

 ## Hartcliffe Health and Environment Action Group

The Gatehouse Centre, Hareclive Road, Hartcliffe, Bristol, BS13 9JN
0117 946 5285
www.hheag.org.uk

Engages residents in health-related and environmental projects.

See case study: 'Health and environment hand in hand' on p. 69.

 ## HorseWorld

Staunton Manor Farm, Staunton Lane, Whitchurch, Bristol, BS14 0QJ
01275 540173
info@horseworld.org.uk
www.horseworld.org.uk

Charity that rescues, rehabilitates and rehomes horses, ponies
and donkeys.

 ## Knowle West Media Centre

Knowle West Media Centre, Leinster Avenue, Knowle West,
Bristol, BS4 1NL
0117 903 0444
projects@kwmc.org.uk
www.kwmc.org.uk

Co-creates projects with local residents to develop their potential.

See case study: 'Supporting grassroots creativity' on p. 70.

 ## Lampton Gardens

Lampton Gardens, off Lampton Avenue, Hartcliffe, Bristol, BS13
0117 964 0114
bristol@csvenvironment.org.uk
www.csv.org.uk

A green space cultivated and cared for by the community.

Malago Valley Conservation Group

Meetings held at: St Peter's Rooms near St Peter's Church, Bishopsworth, Bristol, BS13 8JR
0117 964 3106
info@mvcg.org.uk
www.mvcg.org.uk

Voluntary group working on local conservation issues.

 # The Mede Community Centre

1 Marshall Court, Inns Court, Knowle, Bristol, BS4 1TR
0117 904 1220
themede@hotmail.com
www.themedecommunitycentre.co.uk

Hub of activity for the communities of Inns Court and Knowle West.

 # Open Communication Design

Unit 1.8, Paintworks, Bath Road, Bristol, BS4 3EH
0117 300 5200
info@open-comms.com
www.open-comms.com

Integrated design, branding and social marketing for the digital era.

 # Paintworks Event Space

Paintworks, Bath Road, Bristol, BS4 3EH
0117 971 4320
natalie@paintworksbristol.co.uk
www.paintworksevents.co.uk

An open, versatile space with an exciting programme of events.

At the heart of a sustainable live/work development, this large space is available for hire for weddings, parties, corporate events and exhibitions. The event space also puts on popular public events such as the Love Food Festival and craft shows.

 # The Park Centre

The Park Centre, Daventry Road, Knowle, Bristol, BS4 1DQ
0117 903 9770
joy.pollard@bristol.gov.uk
www.theparkknowle.co.uk

Hub of community activity with business, training and leisure facilities.

Pigeonhouse Stream Park

Off Hawkfield Road, Hartcliffe, Bristol, BS13
info@mvcg.org.uk
www.mvcg.org.uk

Park route following a stream from Hartcliffe towards Hengrove.

 ## Pipeline Spring

Off Daventry Road, Knowle West, Bristol, BS4

Ancient route carrying water down to St Mary Redcliffe church.

Did you know?

Some suburbs are feeling the lack of efficient, affordable public transport, such as Hengrove, where 76% of respondents say they drive to work.

 ## re:store

17 Filwood Broadway, Knowle West, Bristol, BS4 1JL
0117 923 1970
vicky@reworkltd.org.uk
www.reworkltd.org.uk

Repairs and revamps old furniture for sale in the shop and online.

 ## re:work

16 Filwood Broadway, Knowle West, Bristol, BS4 1JL
0117 963 2521
info@reworkltd.org.uk
www.reworkltd.org.uk

Charity training young people and those re-entering employment.

 ## St Anne's Park

Entrance: St Anne's Park Road, Brislington, Bristol, BS4

A popular, formally laid-out park leading to woodland and meadows.

St Anne's Wood and Well

Entrance: St Anne's Park Road, Brislington, Bristol, BS4

A steep, densely wooded valley with a mediaeval well.

 ## T Cup

53-55 Sandy Park Road, Bristol, BS4 3PH
0117 971 9008
info@tcupltd.co.uk
www.tcupltd.co.uk

Relaxed café with top-quality hot drinks and a tantalising menu.

 ## Team FAB

**Meetings held at: The Mede Community and Learning Centre,
1 Marshall Walk, Bristol, BS4 1TR**
07818 262693
projects@kwmc.org.uk
www.kwmc.org.uk

Sewing group raising environmental awareness through their campaign against bags (FAB).

 ## Tree of Life

St Barnabas Church, Daventry Road, Knowle, Bristol, BS4 1DQ
0117 966 4139
agpal46@hotmail.co.uk

Project encouraging Knowle West residents to live sustainably and creatively.

 ## The Tube Diner

Paintworks, Bath Road, Bristol, BS4 3EH
info@thetubediner.co.uk
www.thetubediner.co.uk

Sells fresh sandwiches, drinks and snacks out of an Airstream trailer.

See case study: 'Angie's story' on p. 71.

University of Withywood

131 Queens Road, Withywood, Bristol, BS13 8QD
0117 964 1667
mrsl@blueyonder.co.uk
www.universityofwithywood.org.uk

Charity for local people and educating children in the developing world.

An unusual charity that tries to enhance the quality of life of local people through skills sharing, and raises money for the education of young people in the developing world. Volunteers run a programme of events including language classes, drama, music and discussion groups.

South End fact :

In Brislington, 56% of respondents say they love fresh food and always have their five-a-day.

 # Victory Park

School Road, Brislington, Bristol, BS4

A large neighbourhood park with a semi-rural feel.

 # Wicklea Youth and Community Centre

281 Wick Road, Brislington, Bristol, BS4 4HR
0117 983 7797
info@brislington.org
www.brislington.org/wicklea/index.html

Provides programme of events and activities for local residents.

 # Withywood Centre

Queens Road, Withywood, Bristol, BS13 8QA
0117 987 8400
reception@withywoodcentre.com
www.withywoodcentre.com

Thriving new community centre, health clinic, church and youth café.

Beeses Bar and Tea Gardens

Buzzing away on the river

Beeses Bar and Tea Gardens are hidden in the woods of Eastwood Farm Nature Reserve on the banks of the River Avon. Most people arrive by boat—on Beeses' own ferry, by private boat or on one of the Bristol harbour ferries. Since buying the place in 2006, Phil Leahy and his wife Lindy have refurbished the bar and constructed decking along the waterfront and a marquee for weddings and events. With the help of garden designer Clare McLoughlin they have created lavish flower and herb beds. Open from Easter to September, four days a week, they cope with the busy summer season thanks to their lively team of loyal staff.

Traditionally known for its cream teas, Beeses now has an excellent reputation for its good food. 'Low food miles are important to us when selecting our produce,' Phil explains. 'For example, we buy locally reared Barrow Gurney beef, organic Old Spot sausages and free range chicken.' The beer too is locally sourced including Bath Ales, Butcombe beer and many other Bristol breweries, which are celebrated at Beeses' annual beer festival in September. Good beer and food in an idyllic riverside setting combine well with the Leahys' other passion: music. 'This year,' says Phil, 'we'll be hosting zydeco, blues, funk, brass, a cappella, Country and Western, and classic rock.'

Generations of city dwellers have come to this haven of tranquillity to escape the stresses of city life. It was Anne Beese who first opened the tea gardens in 1846 to serve the railway navvies working on Brunel's new Great Western Railway, which passes through a tunnel close by.

Today, Beeses offers the perfect resting point for walkers, cyclists and groups of school children visiting the nearby Troopers Hill and Eastwood Farm Nature Reserve. The Leahys also support the nature reserve by splitting the proceeds from the beer festival with the Eastwood Farm friends group.

Brislington Community Partnership

Neighbourhood engagement – archaeology to skate parks

Since 1999 the Brislington Community Partnership (BCP) has been funding, guiding, training and linking up local initiatives in Brislington East and West wards. Like a neighbourhood partnership, BCP represents residents in the area and provides resources and back-up for community projects in their early stages. In the first year of council funding, from 2009, BCP awarded more than 25 grants.

Chair David Waters reels off the names of local initiatives the partnership supports, clearly excited by the number of residents keen to improve their neighbourhood. The idea of BCP, he says, is to encourage people in Brislington to engage with each other in developing their community. The Respect project, initiated in 2002, is a good example of this: a breakdown in communication between the older and younger generations led to the 'Big Moan'—a consultation process asking older and younger people what they needed. Two outreach workers were employed by BCP to engage with youth on the streets and out of this came the idea for a skate park and a boxing club at the Wicklea Centre. BCP provided seed funding, and both projects are now running almost independently.

Other groups under the partnership's umbrella include the Friends of Nightingale Valley, and the Arno's Park Action Group, and the Gilton House Tenants Association. BCP have also helped to set up an IT unit in a high-rise block of flats; in the near future, it will be helping to launch an online museum for the Brislington Archaeology Project. The initiatives are diverse and show a wellspring of energy in the neighbourhood.

A key challenge for the partnership is linking Brislington into the rest of south Bristol. Public transport systems currently isolate the area from next door wards. One idea for improving connections is to follow Brislington Brook to its source and link up all the neighbourhoods along the way in a joint effort to clean up the stream. With David's commitment, and that of the dedicated volunteers on his committee, you sense that this, and many other projects, will all be made to happen on the BCP watch.

Buried Treasure Ltd

Greening the city

Buried Treasure Ltd was set up in 2000 by Mil Lusk and Cathi Lillis James—two women with a passion for gardening, teaching and the environment. Based in the Park Centre in Knowle West, this not-for-profit social enterprise helps to green up residents in south Bristol by offering training and support in organic gardening, composting and recycling. Two full-time members of staff and a team of local volunteers and trainees bring these services out to people's gardens, as well as offering workshops in Buried Treasure's own facilities. Their energy and enthusiasm demystifies the move towards organic gardening—and clearly makes it a lot of fun.

Buried Treasure is also linked to other local initiatives that make open spaces around south Bristol greener and more productive. One of these is the Edible Landscapes Movement (ELM), a partnership of neighbourhood groups that develops growing spaces in Knowle West, including the gardens of schools and local residents. 'It's a wonderful grassroots community project,' says Mil. 'Elderly people have given over their gardens to us and we match them up with trainees from the charity re:work, which provides work experience for young people and the unemployed.' Through Mil's independent organisation Green Footprints the movement supplies seedlings to the trainees who grow and harvest the vegetables, then sell them back to ELM for its local veg bag scheme.

Training and education is at the heart of all Buried Treasure's projects. Mil and Cathi recognise the need to help people in their local area develop skills and confidence, which they can go out and use in life. They also teach horticultural skills to teachers and children in local schools, to families and to other charity groups. Working with children, Mil has learned the power of using digital media—a technique widely employed by the Knowle West Media Centre, also part of ELM. 'There's a gap between the old and young in their knowledge and interest in horticulture,' she says. 'But give young people a digital camera and it makes them look more closely: it gets them hooked.'

HHEAG

Health and environment hand in hand

Hartcliffe Health and Environmental Action Group (HHEAG) is based on a housing estate in BS13, recognised by the City Council as an area of multiple deprivation and high health inequalities. The group was set up in 1990 following a survey that asked people in the area how they perceived their well-being. The results showed an urgent need for projects that would help the local population develop a healthy, sustainable lifestyle and local environment.

The HHEAG committee is made up of local residents who have used a community development approach from the start. This method of working encourages, supports and develops residents' abilities to identify issues and to take an active part in bringing about change. The Hartcliffe and Withywood Ramblers is a good example of a successful independent group that was initiated under HHEAG guidance. Other initiatives developed by the group include the Plot to Plate food projects—involving the GREENS community gardens, nutrition and cooking courses, and the Food for All food co-op.

The HHEAG team has learnt a lot along the way. They are now very aware of the importance of taking things slowly, letting things evolve in response to the community's needs, and treating participants as individuals who have valuable skills, knowledge and experience to contribute. Another key part of the group's work has been collaboration with other neighbourhood organisations, such as the Hartcliffe and Withywood Community Partnership, Positive Minds, the Bridge Campus and Hartcliffe and Withywood Ventures. Local residents give their time and commitment to HHEAG projects, and it is their needs and ideas that drive the work carried out.

Like other community groups in Bristol, HHEAG has learned that to create a sustainable neighbourhood people need to work together, listen to each other and value everyone individually. With this strong basis, many future projects are sure to take hold through this action group, which will greatly improve the health and local environment of BS13 residents.

Knowle West Media Centre

Supporting grassroots creativity

A building with a striking eco-design, the Knowle West Media Centre (KWMC) stands out as a beacon in the middle of this sprawling 1930s housing estate. Knowle West was a byword for suburban deprivation by the 1990s, but the Media Centre is bringing change to its social landscape through collaborative film, design and digital media projects that stem from ideas within the community.

The project began in 1996 with an arts and health photography programme launched by the Knowle West Health Association, who appointed Carolyn Hassan as resident photographer and artist. By 2002 KWMC was a registered charity, with Hassan as director. Six years later it moved into a new, purpose-built media centre constructed out of straw bale panels. The design and construction process involved young people and residents at every step to create a building that features natural ventilation, rainwater harvesting, biomass heating and solar panels.

As construction for the new centre went ahead, KWMC launched a new environmental programme, Carbon Makeover. Aimed at engaging people not usually interested in green issues, the programme is a perfect example of the Media Centre's approach: listening to people and using their experiences to create platforms for new ideas and social change. Four social enterprises have so far emerged out of the scheme, along with numerous small success stories: a resident who rewrote the instructions on an energy meter so others could understand them; another who saw that the estate was a 'food desert' and so launched a fruit and veg stall.

The centre also works with artists to develop ideas about how to make the community greener. The Harrisons Studio, for example, from California, developed the concept of an open canopy forest as a piece of public art, which would sequester carbon and provide socialising travel routes around the Knowle West estate. These collaborative projects drive the work that comes out of KWMC and ensures ongoing innovative programmes that bring together practitioners and the community.

The Tube Diner

Angie's story

Since 2009, Angie Holland has spent her days fulfilling her life ambition.
With a deep-rooted love of food she is now running one of the funkiest
cafés in Bristol, in the cool creative quarter of the Paintworks. The Tube
Diner consists of two retro, chrome Airstream trailers, one for cooking and
one for eating, which fit perfectly in a spot near the Paintworks entrance.
The Diner, described in a sign on site as a 'micro café, serving hot and
cold drinks, snacks, grills, homemade cakes and other essentials', is
definitely worth heading for. The food is fresh and tasty, and the eating
trailer is a true 1950s American diner experience with ice cream parlour
bar stools, red vinyl booth seats and boomerang Formica tables.

The idea to run a café had been part of Angie's plans for a while. When
the Paintworks site was starting to re-emerge from its industrial past in the
mid-2000s she met Ashley Nicholson, one of the developers, and talked
to him about building a home and running a business there. At the time,
as a food technology teacher, she was keen to make the break from one
profession to another. Ashley was very supportive and once Angie's loft
apartment was completed he suggested there was a need for an informal
café at the Paintworks. They worked together to make the idea of the
Tube Diner happen.

Now, with a strong following of regular customers, the passion Angie
has for her small business shines through. The environmental aspects of
catering are core to her philosophy. This includes reducing packaging as
much as possible and only wrapping sandwiches in waxed paper. She is
also doing some guerrilla gardening on the side, and her rows of lettuces
and courgettes are finding their way into the diner's food.

Angie is well known around the Paintworks. She sends out a weekly
newsletter with her 'rantings', as she calls them, and for the Diner's first
birthday she put together an 'Annual' with the best stories, rantings,
photos and recipes from the year. With the diner so well established she
now has plans to develop a new type of sandwich service, and to set up
a catering business and cookery school. The empire of Angie expands.

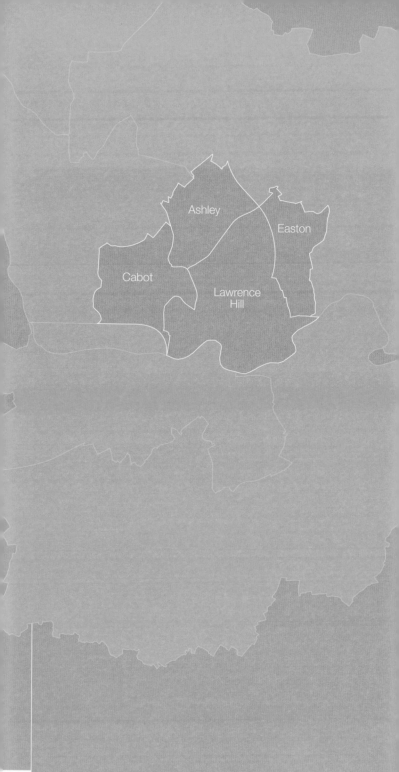

Ashley

Easton

Cabot

Lawrence
Hill

East Central

The neighbourhoods making up East Central defy the usual pigeonholing. The area stretches from St Pauls, near the city centre, out to Easton across the M32 and around to St Phillips, tucked behind Brunel's Temple Meads station.

These are the most multi-cultural communities in Bristol, where you will find grassroots gardening projects, cutting-edge eco-architectural businesses and social enterprises supporting international development. Each group has a message for sustainable living and caring for the environment in ways that are innovative, fun and make good sense.

St Pauls was built in Georgian times, leaving a legacy of grand buildings and squares that now host a dynamic, culturally diverse neighbourhood. Its annual street carnival is one of the highlights of the city's calendar. Its neighbour, Montpelier, has a thriving eco-community where the Transition Towns movement has a large and growing following. Old Market and St Phillips, dissected by waterways, have remained intact despite new constructions going up and old buildings coming down. The start of Sustran's Bristol to Bath cycle path can be found hiding behind industrial warehouse units here.

St Werburghs is best known for its green and secluded city farm and the organic supermarket, the Better Food Company. Across the M32, Easton has the rich, multi-ethnic atmosphere of St Mark's Road and the Eastside Roots garden centre by the railway line. East Central is definitely alive and kicking, with good living taking off in all directions. This energy is rippling into smaller pockets as the enthusiasm for doing things in new and better ways becomes contagious.

St Pauls Carnival

Stroll around the eastside

Strolling along the streets of this area gives you a good feel for its diverse culture and history. The tour starts out in Montpelier at the Radford Mill Farm Shop, which is part of the fabric of this alternative residential neighbourhood. Walking from here to St Pauls you pass rows of terraced Victorian houses before entering streets from the Georgian era, best preserved in the impressive Portland Square.

Heading from St Pauls into St Werburghs you come to the Better Food Company's eco-store and café, selling every organic product you can imagine. In the same building the Children's Scrapstore is a fun place to hunt around for colourful materials for kids' parties. Further on, in the heart of St Werburghs, is a very unexpected find: a climbing wall in an old church. Undercover Rock have developed this centre by tapping into the demand among urban-based climbers to scale a peak or two.

The tour then takes you through a tunnel to the quiet seclusion of the city farm, a favourite place for small children and parents alike, with the greenery of the Ashley Vale allotments all around. Just across the road is the eco-home self-build development of the Ashley Vale Action Group, which is well worth investigating.

Walking this tour will take an hour or so if you need to be fast. But it could also take three hours if you spend time looking at everything the area has to offer.

 ## Where to start

Radford Mill Farm Shop is on Picton Street, a 30-minute walk from Temple Meads station or a ten-minute walk from the city centre. The tour can easily be cycled as well. Car parking is limited in this inner city area.

For more travel information please refer to pp. 16–17.

1 Radford Mill Farm Shop

41 Picton Street, Montpelier, Bristol, BS6 5PZ

Organic wholefood shop with a tea room and deli.

A mainstay of Montpelier residents for years, this shops sells organic vegetables from the Radford Mill farm as well as handmade arts and crafts and books. Its café is a good stopping-off place if you've been shopping nearby. Just next door is La Freak Boutique—a treasure trove for vintage clothes lovers.

Turning right out of the farm shop take the first right by the Thali Café into Wellington Avenue. Turn right into Ashley Road and take the first left into Brigstocke Road. Follow this street down five blocks to Portland Square.

East Central fact :

Montpelier, St Pauls and St Werburghs are packed full with artistic types—52% of respondents there have taken part in creative activities in the past year.

2 Portland Square

Historic Georgian square in the middle of St Pauls.

A secluded spot with trees and rose bushes in the central garden and five-storey Georgian buildings around the sides. On the north-east side, the newly restored St Pauls church is now home to Circomedia. Across the square in the basement is Cosies Wine Bar, the renowned late-night hang out.

Head back up Brigstocke Road and take the first right into Grosvenor Road. St Pauls Learning and Family Centre is several streets down here on the right.

St Pauls Learning and Family Centre

94 Grosvenor Road, St Pauls, Bristol, BS2 8XJ

Community centre with a library, café, training rooms and hall.

A fantastic resource containing a public library, two large art studios, music rooms, darkroom facilities and a café. The centre also allows local agencies to use the space to provide training for local residents, support the unemployed in finding work, and help children do their homework.

Continue on to the end of Grosvenor Road. Where it comes out on Ashley Road head straight on and turn left at the traffic lights into Sussex Place. A few minutes further on, take a right at the roundabout onto Sevier Street and the Better Food Company is just there on the left.

The Better Food Company

The Bristol Proving House, Sevier Street, Bristol, BS2 9QS

Enterprise making organic food more widely available.

See case study: 'Reconnecting the plate to the plot' on p. 95.

The Children's Scrapstore is above the Better Food Company. It is accessed round the side, through the car park.

Children's Scrapstore

Scrapstore House, 21 Sevier Street, St Werburghs, Bristol, BS2 9LB

Best place in town for creative materials for children's workshops.

This long-standing Bristol charity provides a low-cost creative resource for its member groups by collecting safe waste from businesses. It stocks all sorts of materials for creative play, such as paper and card, foam, plastic pots, tubs, fabric and piles of off-cuts and leftovers.

Continue along Sevier Street and turn left at the mini roundabout into Mina Road. The Undercover Rock Climbing Centre is four blocks up here on the right, inside the church.

Undercover Rock Climbing Centre

St Werburghs Church, Mina Road, St Werburghs, Bristol, BS2 9YT

One of the most comprehensive indoor climbing facilities in the UK.

This climbing centre has an original setting in an old church. The space is used to great effect to house walls suitable for beginners as well as the most experienced climbers. Courses for all levels run throughout the year, both in the centre and outdoors.

Head through the tunnel outside the climbing centre. Where the road forks, go left up Watercress Road and the city farm entrance is at the top on the left.

 St Werburghs City Farm

Watercress Road, Bristol, BS2 9YJ

Exemplary city farm working in partnership with the local community.

This much-loved farm inspires and educates members of the local community with its work. A livestock holding and community garden, it offers training to adults as well as the Boiling Wells youth work project. An independent café next door sells excellent, original dishes using sustainable ingredients that include produce from the farm.

Go back down Watercress Road and turn left into Mina Road, then immediately right into the Yard. This is the eco-home self-build site of the Ashley Vale Action Group.

 Ashley Vale Action Group

228 Mina Road, St Werburghs, Bristol, BS2 9YP

Residents' group that has developed a self-build site.

See case study: 'Scaffolding yard to eco self-builds' on p. 94.

To head back into town, make your way back to the Better Food Company. There is a bus stop here on Sevier Street.

Cycle around the eastside

This tour takes in part of the UK's first ever cycle route—the Bristol to Bath Railway Path—and large areas of east central Bristol. It starts behind Brunel's Temple Meads station at the Bristol Wood Recycling Project, which uses a once derelict site to sell a range of old timbers and beautifully crafted furniture. From here the route passes the Dings home zone near the Temple Quay business area on its way to the Bristol SOFA Project. A visionary initiative, SOFA has provided many an affordable table and chair while removing thousands of tonnes of furniture from landfill.

A quick cycle takes you to the start of the Bristol to Bath Railway Path. This first stretch meanders through Lawrence Hill and Easton and, after 15 minutes of traffic-free bliss, arrives at an exit right beside Greenbank Cemetery. This is a peaceful green space to rest and recharge your cycling legs. The tour then heads off through Easton's streets to St Mark's Road, where two eateries well worth stopping for are the award-winning Café Maitreya and one of the much-loved Thali Cafés. From here, visit the inspiring Eastside Roots community gardening project nearby before heading back via Easton's Community Centre.

Cycling this tour will take an hour and a half to enjoy all the sights. If you'd rather walk it would take twice as long, depending on your pace.

 ## Where to start

The Bristol Wood Recycling Project is behind Temple Meads station on the Sustrans National Cycle Route 3, the West Country Way. Many of the places can be reached by bus if you want to visit just a few at a time.

For more travel information please refer to pp. 16–17.

Café Maitreya

1 Bristol Wood Recycling Project

13 Cattle Market Road, St Philips, Bristol, BS1 6QW

Saves wood from landfill and provides affordable timber to the public.

This social enterprise saves wood from becoming waste, recycles it and sells it back to the public at affordable prices. It has a collection service, timber yard and a workshop selling beautifully crafted wood products. It also offers a range of volunteer and work placement opportunities.

Turn left onto Cattle Market Road and carry on until the traffic lights, turning left here into Avon Road. Carry on to take a right in front of the Ibis Hotel and then directly left into Anvil Street, taking a right at the end onto Horton Street. To reach the SOFA Project turn left at the Midland Road junction and then immediately right onto Waterloo Road. Take the next left into Waterloo Street to reach West Street where you'll find the project's shop front.

2 SOFA Project Bristol

48-54 West Street, St Philips, Bristol, BS2 0BL

Supplies second-hand household goods at low prices.

See case study: 'Giving value and reducing waste' on p. 98.

Go back to Waterloo Road and follow it to the end to take a right onto Trinity Street. You'll see the start of the Bristol to Bath Railway Path on your left, framed by the first of many pieces of public art along the route.

I ♥ Bristol because...
we have more street parties than anywhere else in the UK.

③ Bristol and Bath Railway Path

Cycle path, starts at Trinity Street, St Philips, Bristol, BS2

Off-road route open to walkers, cyclists and disabled users.

A 13-mile off-road route starting in St Phillips, the Bristol and Bath Railway Path is popular with both walkers and cyclists, many commuting between the two cities. It has inspired over a dozen artworks, which are installed along the route, and it also functions as an important wildlife corridor.

Follow the path through the neighbourhoods of Lawrence Hill and Easton until you reach a turn-off for Greenbank Road. Once off the path enter the cemetery by following Greenbank Road around for a little while to the left.

④ Greenbank Cemetery

Greenbank Road, Easton, Bristol, BS5 6HL

Oasis of calm in the middle of Easton.

Easily accessible from the Bristol and Bath Railway Path, this is a picturesque Victorian cemetery with listed monuments and a small derelict chapel. A quiet expanse of green, the cemetery also contains memorials to the civilians killed in the Bristol Blitz of 1941, and a military quarter with many decorated graves.

Follow through the cemetery to come out on Greenbank View. Turn left to reach Robertson Road. After passing a number of roads on your left turn into Belle Vue Road. Take the first right into Mivart Street and then at the junction with St Mark's Road turn right to see Café Maitreya on the left ahead of you.

⑤ Café Maitreya

89 St Mark's Road, Easton, Bristol, BS5 6HY

One of the UK's most highly acclaimed vegetarian restaurants.

'*Maitreya*' means loving kindness or universal love in Sanskrit—values that the café reflects in its food. Judged by the Vegetarian Society as the top vegetarian restaurant in the country, it prides itself on a sumptuous seasonal menu that changes regularly. Ingredients are sourced from local, small-scale and ethical producers.

From the café entrance turn right into St Mark's Road until you reach the signs to Stapleton Road train station. Follow these signs up towards the platform and you'll see the Eastside Roots Garden Centre there on your left.

⑥ Eastside Roots

Next to Stapleton Road Station, Easton, Bristol, BS16 1AU

Community gardening hub for Easton and the wider Bristol community.

See case study: 'Growing food and communities' on p. 97.

From the garden centre head back down to St Mark's Road, turning right towards the Sugar Loaf pub. As St Mark's Road bends round to the right, follow on ahead into Albion Road and Chelsea Road, all the way to the Easton Community Centre at the end.

⑦ Easton Community Centre

Kilburn Street, Easton, Bristol, BS5 6AW

Communal social space for events and learning opportunities.

In the heart of Easton the community centre puts on a range of activities for people of all ages and from all backgrounds. It also has a children's play area, internet access and a meeting room. Easton residents can hire the building for children's parties or the sports area for five-a-side games.

Just after the Easton Community Centre cross over Easton Road and continue straight ahead to find your way back onto the Bristol and Bath Railway Path. Here you can either go back to the start of the path or carry on all the way to Bath.

Directory

 ## Ashley Vale Action Group

228 Mina Road, St Werburghs, Bristol, BS2 9YP
07773 370698
avag@ashleyvale.org.uk
www.ashleyvale.org.uk

Residents' group that has developed a self-build site.

See case study: 'Scaffolding yard to eco self-builds' on p. 94.

 ## Ashley Vale Allotments Association

Watercress Road, St Werburghs, Bristol, BS2 9YJ
www.ashleyvaleallotmentsassociation.org

Provides land for growing food, promoting healthy living and
conserving wildlife.

 ## Baggator

The Pickle Factory, 13 All Hallows Road, Bristol, BS5 0HH
0117 955 7733
do-it@baggator.org
www.baggator.org

Programmes to inspire young people to fulfil their potential.

An Easton-based project providing programmes of non-formal education,
skills training and leisure activities for young people. Its aim is to inspire
participants to discover their potential and support the journey from
childhood curiosity to adult responsibility in ways that are accessible
and fun.

Radford Mill Farm Shop

 ## Barton Hill Settlement

43 Ducie Road, Barton Hill, Bristol, BS5 0AX
0117 955 6971
admin@bartonhillsettlement.org.uk
www.bartonhillsettlement.org.uk

Provides services and facilities to residents in the surrounding area.

A community resource centre and independent charity, the Barton Hill Settlement is a driving force for development in the area. It provides a wide range of courses and assistance for local people, such as the Over 50s Project, youth clubs, a family play centre and community work.

 ## The Better Food Company

The Bristol Proving House, Sevier Street, Bristol, BS2 9QS
0117 935 1725
admin@betterfood.co.uk
www.betterfood.co.uk

Enterprise making organic food more widely available.

See case study: 'Reconnecting the plate to the plot' on p. 95.

 ## Box Architecture

127 Wilder Street, St Pauls, Bristol, BS2 8QU
0117 914 5204
office@boxarchitecture.co.uk
www.boxarchitecture.co.uk

Sustainable design services for masterplanning, architecture and interior design.

Brana Design

228 Mina Road, St Werburghs, Bristol, BS2 9YP
0117 924 7325
paulbranamartin@gmail.com
www.branadesign.com

Environmentally conscious architectural services from concept through to project management.

 ## Bristol and Bath Railway Path

Cycle path, starts at Trinity Street, St Philips, Bristol, BS2
0117 922 3719
bristolparks@bristol.gov.uk
www.bristolbathrailwaypath.org.uk

An off-road route open to walkers, cyclists and disabled users.

 ## Bristol Community Transport

185-189 Easton Road, Easton, Bristol, BS5 0HQ
0117 902 0157
office@bristolcommunitytransport.org.uk
www.bristolcommunitytransport.org.uk

Fleet of minibuses for use by community groups and not-for-profit organisations.

 ## Bristol Food Hub

95 Mina Road, St Werburghs, Bristol, BS2 9XP
07886 807048
rachel@bristolfoodhub.org
www.bristolfoodhub.org

Works with communities to make our food culture more people and planet friendly.

 ## Bristol Wood Recycling Project

13 Cattle Market Road, St Philips, Bristol, BS1 6QW
0117 972 3219
www.bwrp.org.uk

Saves wood from landfill and provides affordable timber to the public.

 ## Café Kino

3 Ninetree Hill, Bristol, BS1 3SB
0117 924 9200
eat@cafe-kino.com
www.cafe-kino.com

Not-for-profit café cooperative owned and run by its workers.

 ## Café Maitreya

89 St Mark's Road, Easton, Bristol, BS5 6HY
0117 951 0100
thesnug@cafemaitreya.co.uk
www.cafemaitreya.co.uk

One of the UK's most highly acclaimed vegetarian restaurants.

 ## Children's Scrapstore

Scrapstore House, 21 Sevier Street, St Werburghs, Bristol, BS2 9LB
0117 908 5644
coordinator@childrensscrapstore.co.uk
www.childrensscrapstore.co.uk

Best place in town for creative materials for children's workshops.

 ## Circomedia

St Pauls Church, Portland Square, Bristol, BS2 8SJ
0117 924 7615
info@circomedia.com
www.circomedia.com

A leading centre in Europe for contemporary circus with physical theatre.

 ## Easton and Lawrence Hill Neighbourhood Management

108 Church Road, Redfield, Bristol, BS5 9LJ
0117 903 9975
officemanager@eastonandlawrencehill.org.uk
www.eastonandlawrencehill.org.uk

Community partnership providing advice and information on local services.

Easton Community Allotment

18 Eve Road, Easton, Bristol, BS5 0JX
eastoncommallot@yahoo.com
www.myspace.com/eastoncommunityallotment

Social space where people can learn to grow their own food.

Easton Community Centre

Kilburn Street, Easton, Bristol, BS5 6AW
0117 954 1409
info@eastoncommunitycentre.org.uk

Communal social space for events and learning opportunities.

Easton Energy Group

36 Britannia Road, Easton, Bristol, BS5 6DA
easton.energy.group@gmail.com
www.eastonenergygroup.org

Gives free advice on ways to reduce energy consumption and bills.

Eastside Roots

Next to Stapleton Road Station, Easton, Bristol, BS16 1AU
07810 806354
enquiries@eastsideroots.org.uk
eastsideroots.org.uk

Community gardening hub for Easton and the wider Bristol community.

See case study: 'Growing food and communities' on p. 97.

Eco Village Network UK

10-12 Picton Street, Montpelier, Bristol, BS6 5QA
0117 944 6219
www.evnuk.org.uk

Information resource and news service promoting sustainable settlement.

FRANK Water

Unit 2B, Wellington Lane, Bristol, BS6 5PY
0117 329 4846
katie@frankwater.com
www.frankwater.com

Sells bottled water to fund clean water projects in developing countries.

Friends of the Earth – Bristol

10-12 Picton Street, Montpelier, Bristol, BS6 5QA
0117 911 4084 (voicemail)
www.bristolfoe.org.uk

Very active local group of the international environmental organisation.

See case study: 'Acting together' on p. 96.

 ## Greenbank Cemetery

Greenbank Road, Easton, Bristol, BS5 6HL

Oasis of calm in the middle of Easton.

 ## Green Hat Graphic Design

Studio 2 St Andrews Rd, Bristol, BS6 5EH
0117 330 0768
team@greenhatdesign.co.uk
www.greenhatdesign.co.uk

Graphic design company with high environmental standards.

 ## Green Source Solutions

14 Kingsland Trading Estate, St Phillips Road, Bristol, BS2 0JZ
0117 304 2390
recycling@greensource.co.uk
www.greensource.co.uk

Charity reducing waste by re-manufacturing old printer cartridges and mobile phones.

 ## GROFUN

Hopetoun Road, St Werburghs, Bristol, BS2 9YL
07973 847894
info@grofun.org.uk
www.grofun.org.uk

Not-for-profit organisation helping people grow food.

GROFUN (Growing Real Organic Food in Urban Neighbourhoods) was set up in 2006 to improve the public's access to fresh, organic food. It teaches people to grow their own food, no matter how little space they have, and works with schools to help children take pleasure and pride in producing their own vegetables.

Imagination Solar Ltd

Unit 4 Montpelier Central, Station Road, Montpelier, Bristol, BS6 5EE
0117 942 6668
enquiries@imaginationsolar.com
www.imaginationsolar.com

Business offering simple, effective solar systems at affordable prices.

I♥ Bristol because...
I love the piglets in the city farms.

Kebele Community Coop

14 Robertson Road, Bristol, BS5 6JY
0117 951 3086
kebelesocialcentre@riseup.net
www.kebelecoop.org

Community cooperative providing an alternative social space.

La Freak Boutique

47 Picton Street, Montpelier, Bristol, BS6 5PZ
07973 854965
www.lafreakboutique.co.uk

Montpelier's funky vintage and second-hand clothes shop.

Labour Behind the Label

10-12 Picton Street, Bristol, BS6 5QA
0117 944 1700
info@labourbehindthelabel.org
www.labourbehindthelabel.org

Supporting garment workers worldwide, defending their rights and improving working conditions.

 **Living Easton**

5 Ashman Close, Easton, Bristol, BS5 0RQ
0117 955 9817
mjbaker1066@yahoo.co.uk

Community organisation celebrating Easton's diversity of cultures.

 Love Easton

shankari@hotmail.com
www.loveeaston.com

Pioneering community group creating a shared vision for Easton.

An innovative volunteer group made up of local residents from the Easton area who share the goal of ensuring creative, community-led development for Easton and Lawrence Hill.

 Mivart Street Studios

Mivart Street, Easton, Bristol, BS5 6JL
info@mivartartists.co.uk
www.mivartartists.co.uk

Workspaces for applied artists, musicians, street theatre and circus groups.

 Narroways Millennium Green Trust

C/o St Werburghs City Farm, Watercress Road, St Werburghs, Bristol, BS2 9YJ
07907 841238
narroways@netscape.net
http://freespace.virgin.net/harry.jen

A grassy, wooded ridge preserved for wildlife.

 Portishead Press Ltd

Unit 8, Circuit 32, Easton Road, Bristol, BS5 0DB
0117 955 5811
www.portisheadpress.co.uk

Family-run print media company with high environmental credentials.

Radford Mill Farm Shop

41 Picton Street, Montpelier, Bristol, BS6 5PZ
0117 942 6644

Organic wholefood shop with a tea room and deli.

 ## Silai for Skills

176 Easton Rd, Easton, Bristol, BS5 0EF
0117 941 5180
info@silai.org.uk
www.silai.org.uk

Charitable college helping women increase their confidence and skills.

A female-only sewing project that supports women and develops
their skills through learning. It offers many different courses including
alterations, general sewing, and textile craft and design. Courses are
aimed at all levels, from beginners through to experienced craftswomen.

 ## SOFA Project Bristol

48-54 West Street, St Philips, Bristol, BS2 0BL
0117 954 3567
info@sofaproject.org.uk
www.sofaproject.org.uk

Supplies second-hand household goods at low prices.

See case study: 'Giving value and reducing waste' on p. 98.

 ## St Pauls Learning and Family Centre

94 Grosvenor Road, St Pauls, Bristol, BS2 8XJ
0117 914 5470
stpaulslearningcentre.reception@bristol.gov.uk
www.bristol.gov.uk

Community centre with a library, café, training rooms and hall.

 ## St Pauls Unlimited

St Agnes Lodge, Thomas Street, Bristol, BS2 9LJ
0117 903 9934
spu@bristol.gov.uk
stpaulsunlimited.wordpress.com

Community-led organisation advocating and lobbying for St Pauls.

St Werburghs City Farm

Watercress Road, Bristol, BS2 9YJ
0117 942 8241
office@swcityfarm.co.uk
www.swcityfarm.org.uk

Exemplary city farm working in partnership with the local community.

 ## St Werburghs Community Website

St Werburghs Neighbourhood Association, C/o St Werburghs
Community Centre, Horley Road, Bristol, BS2 9TJ
information@stwerburghs.org
www.stwerburghs.org

Community website highlighting what's going on in the area.

 ## Sweet Mart

80 St Mark's Road, Easton, Bristol, BS5 6JH
0117 951 2257
www.sweetmart.co.uk

An Asian Aladdin's cave of fresh produce and groceries with a deli.

 ## Thali Café

12 York Road, Bristol, BS6 5QE
0117 951 4979
www.thethalicafe.co.uk

Quirky vegetarian restaurant serving Indian street food on a tin plate.

This is the first of four Thali Cafés (others in Totterdown, Easton and
Clifton). With just two choices on the menu, its dishes are fresh, tasty and
good value, using seasonal and organic ingredients. The café is a cosy,
friendly, happy place, but you can also join the tiffin club and take your
meal home.

 ## Timber Routes

42 Armoury Square, Easton, Bristol, BS5 0PT
0117 903 9775
info@timber-routes.co.uk
www.timber-routes.co.uk

Designs and manufactures quality mortise-and-tenon timber frames.

Transition Easton

transitioneaston@yahoo.co.uk
www.transitioneaston.org.uk

Works with the community to create a sustainable, oil-free future.

 ## Transition Montpelier

www.transitionmontpelier.org.uk

Working to reduce the community's carbon footprint and oil dependence.

 ## The Trinity Centre

Trinity Road, Bristol, BS2 0NW
0117 935 1200
info@3ca.org.uk
http://3ca.org.uk

Community-run space hosting a range of imaginative activities.

Managed by a community association and located in a beautiful old church in Lawrence Hill, the Trinity Centre puts on a diverse range of activities from art projects to reggae revivals, music performances and firework celebrations. It also offers a wide variety of training courses for young people and adult learners.

 ## Undercover Rock Climbing Centre

St Werburghs Church, Mina Road, St Werburghs, Bristol, BS2 9YT
0117 941 3489
enquiries@undercover-rock.com
www.undercover-rock.com

One of the most comprehensive indoor climbing facilities in the UK.

Wellspring Healthy Living Centre

Beam Street, Barton Hill, Bristol, BS5 9QY
0117 304 1400
reception@wellspringhlc.org
www.wellspringhlc.org

Integrated medical centre with complementary therapies, arts projects and a kitchen.

See case study: 'Holistic community well-being' on p. 99.

 **White Design**

The Proving House, 21 Sevier Street, St Werburghs, Bristol, BS2 9LB
0117 954 7333
mail@white-design.co.uk
http://white-design.co.uk

Architectural practice and sustainability consultancy.

 Did you know?

The global issue of climate change has some local residents
concerned. In Easton, 40% of respondents are very worried
about the impact it will have on the UK.

Wild Goose Space

The Yard, 228 Mina Road, Bristol, BS2 9YP
07773 370698
wildegoosespace@ashleyvale.org.uk
www.wildgoosespace.org.uk

Room in the Yard available for hire by the community.

Ashley Vale Action Group

Scaffolding yard to eco self-builds

Ashley Vale is a green, secluded neighbourhood enclosed by steep wooded embankments and allotment-covered hillsides. Its mix of housing, workshops, city farm, café, pub and community-developed gardens makes it an enviable place in which to live. The Ashley Vale Action Group (AVAG) was formed in 2000 by local residents concerned about the re-development of a former scaffolding yard in the vale. Forming a not-for-profit company they raised money to buy the land and pushed forward their alternative proposal of turning it into a self-build site. The land was divided into plots and sold to individuals who supported the aim of developing innovative, ecological housing and who valued the importance of working with the surrounding community.

Ten years on, the homes are all built and occupied, each one with its own distinctive timber-framed design. A central green is open to all residents, and the ground floor of the last building to be developed (a renovated office block) remains in the ownership of AVAG. The Wild Goose Space is located here—a room available for community members to hire—alongside three work units with long-term tenants: a group of artists, a female creative cooperative and a self-build consultancy.

The Better Food Company

Reconnecting the plate to the plot

In a renovated industrial unit on St Werburghs' main road is a treasure
trove of organic, local and fairtraded food. It's hard to pass by the door
without being tempted in to buy the ingredients for your next meal or
indulge in a dish freshly cooked at the café. This is the Better Food
Company, an organic supermarket, café, wholesale business and veg box
scheme. The brainchild of managing director Phil Haughton, the company
is driven by a belief in the need to reconnect consumers with ethically and
sustainably produced food. Located in the inner city, it is directly linked to
farmers and growers in the countryside around.

Haughton is passionate about organic food and farming, having worked
on a community farm in Scotland as a young adult and been involved in
Bristol's Windmill Hill City Farm in the early 1980s. He first started selling
organic produce in the Gloucester Road in 1985, then moved the
business to St Werburghs, running it initially as a delivery service. The
retail outlet established in 2002 sells environmentally friendly household
goods, health and beauty products, books and gifts as well as food.
More recently, Haughton helped to found the Community Farm in Chew
Magna—25 acres of prime organic land just outside Bristol—which now
supplies much of the shop's fresh produce.

The Better Food Company is more, then, than just the building you see
on Sevier Street. Beyond the business side it works hard to highlight
the links between farmer and consumer, between soil, plants, animals
and man, and to challenge the conventional food system and its
unsustainable practices. It also works with schools to teach children
the joys of cooking and eating fresh, organically grown produce.
And Haughton is an advisor to several local enterprises and
community organisations.

There are plans to open another Better Food Company shop in Bristol and
to continue providing outreach support where needed. When asked how
we can make Bristol a better place to live, Haughton replies, 'We're doing
a good job already, but perhaps more collaboration is needed between
diverse groups and people. Diversity and connection are the key.'

Bristol Friends of the Earth

Acting together

Bristol Friends of the Earth (BFoE) was formed in 1971 as part of a nationwide, European and international network of FoE groups. Their launch event involved dumping non-returnable bottles at Schweppes' offices in Brislington—a stunt carried out by the first eight local FoE groups in the country. BFoE often works in alliances, forming campaign groups such as Stop Bristol Airport Expansion, which has held up the airport's plans for growth for the past four years, and BAMBI (Bristol Against Mass Burn Incineration), in opposition to a mass-burn incinerator contract for disposing of the West of England's domestic waste. The group is also part of ACSEB (Action for Sustainable Energy for Bristol), which, so far, has held off the construction of a palm-oil burning power station for Avonmouth. With the support of many Bristol residents, BFoE has also lobbied Bristol City Council to support FoE's nationwide campaign 'Get Serious about CO_2'. This, in part, led to the council passing a motion in November 2009 that committed the city to making a 40 per cent reduction in CO_2 emissions by 2020.

In line with the national group, BFoE tries to equip people in Bristol with skills to develop their own campaigns in response to local issues that concern them. Aware that some people are intimidated by the idea of campaigning, FoE's idea of the campaign postcard is an effective way to get them started. Individuals can encourage friends to sign a postcard about a particular issue, collect these postcards, and then start lobbying the City Council or the UK or European parliaments. This was FoE's method for starting campaigns that led to the Doorstep Recycling Act—committing councils in England to collecting at least two recyclable items from your doorstep—and the Climate Change Act, which commits the UK to tough CO_2 emission reduction targets. In Bristol, the mass protest supported by BFoE against plans to turn the Bristol to Bath cycle path into a Bus Rapid Transit route shows that small actions by many individuals can help to bring about a real change.

Eastside Roots

Growing food and communities

Eastside Roots is a vibrant community garden set up in 2007 on the site of an old railway station at Stapleton Road. Initial funding from Bristol City Council and Bristol Eastside Traders established the project, and now local people give their time on a voluntary basis, which has led to greater support and cooperation between members. The site is being developed as a community-led garden centre, following a social enterprise model that is financially sustainable yet benefits its members and the wider community. It stocks a wide range of plants but focuses mainly on those that are edible or good for the local ecology.

Eastside Roots also helps manage the garden at the Trinity Centre, another place for a spot of good living. These gardening hubs provide a social space where people can connect with the land while becoming more integrated into their community. At Stapleton Road the timber-framed eco-building with a living roof is a popular venue for celebrations, live music gigs and arts festivals, as well as a great space for hosting training sessions. The project currently offers workshops and short courses in horticulture, which equip people with knowledge and skills to start growing food and other plants in their own gardens, backyards or even window boxes. The garden also becomes an outdoor classroom for educational events for adults and local schools.

Members of Eastside Roots particularly value the connections that the project has made with other organisations in the area, including the Bristol Permaculture Group, local refugee and asylum seeker programmes and the City Council's youth funding team. They are currently planning further developments of the site to improve the quality of their services and to offer skills and labour to help households set up their own gardens.

SOFA Project Bristol

Giving value and reducing waste

Based in the heart of Old Market the SOFA Project Bristol is a major centre for the reuse and recycling of unwanted furniture. Since 1980 it has grown from one man with a van to a large organisation with multiple sites. Unwanted furniture of all types is picked up by volunteers, reconditioned and then resold at bargain prices. Each year the project collects around 8,000 items, thereby saving 600 tonnes from landfill and helping 5,000 families acquire good value furniture. As well as its store in Old Market it has outlets in Knowle (for higher-end products) and in Weston-super-Mare. The stores are open to everyone, and there are discounts for customers on low incomes and benefits.

The SOFA Project intends to expand to provide recycled bicycles and reconditioned office furniture for use by charities. In the meantime, it has broadened the scope of its work to include the promotion of a socially responsible attitude towards waste, and to retrain prisoners with useful skills. It teaches those on day release from Leyhill Prison to restore furniture so they can build up real qualifications and work towards a fresh start. As well as paid staff the project has a number of volunteers and employs people as part of the Future Jobs Fund.

Julian Williams, director of the SOFA Project, has found the experience of developing these programmes immensely rewarding, particularly working with prisoners. He also says that realising how effective reuse can be in tackling the city's environmental challenges has been 'a revelation'. So, if you're looking for some new furniture, the SOFA Project is not just a financially sound choice with its low prices and lack of VAT, but also an environmentally and ethically great option.

Wellspring Health Centre

Holistic community well-being

The stained glass windows around the entrance immediately suggest that this is a health centre with a difference. The artworks, architectural design and kitchen garden are all part of the holistic approach to health undertaken at the Wellspring Healthy Living Centre (WHLC). The focus here is on improving the well-being of individuals through looking after both their physical and mental health. Working like this across the generations is seen as key to building a healthier community in general.

Wellspring offers all the mainstream health services—GP surgery, dentist, pharmacy, health visitors—and complements these with alternative therapies and courses in healthy living. Local residents can take their children to the homeopathy clinic, or attend a course in family cooking, take part in an art and textile workshop, or sing in a small choir. The long list of activities and services available is geared towards all members of the community, whether young, old, physically disabled or with learning disabilities. The success of this approach was recognised by a national good practice award in 2005, presented by the Prince of Wales.

The range of services on offer is impressive, but the story of how the WHLC came into being is also noteworthy. In 2000 local residents formed the action group Healthy Places Happy People and acquired funding from the ten-year regeneration programme for this area of Bristol to develop a new health centre—one that locals could be proud of. Under the management of the registered charity Community at Heart a building was constructed with a unique environmental design, which won the WHLC a Civic Society Award in 2004. The seven artworks commissioned for the entrance area—including the gates, a limestone sculpture in the courtyard and floor mosaics in the reception—make the centre stand out.

Today, Wellspring is a charity in its own right run by a board of trustees, the majority of whom are local residents. It works in collaboration with many community groups, the City Council and the NHS to extend the use of its services across the whole of Bristol. You don't have to live in this area in order to make use of the facilities.

Central Bristol

Central

Bristol's buzzing central area draws in workers, students, shoppers and tourists alike. With its combination of harbour and hills, ancient streets and modern developments, it is an intriguing and exciting place to explore.

Tucked away in the old town, St Nicholas Market is home to the largest collection of independent retailers in Bristol, and right next door, in Corn Street, is the renowned weekly Farmers Market. Just down the road, Bristol's historic floating harbour is the backdrop to flagship attractions such as Brunel's ss Great Britain, At Bristol science museum and the Watershed media centre, which plays host to the international Wildscreen film festival.

Built out of the riches once generated by the port, Queen Square, green and magnificent, has long been the city's financial heart as well as a site of historic social unrest. Today, this central area is home to major national players in the sustainability sector including the Soil Association, Sustrans and the Environment Agency.

Central Bristol also encompasses a plethora of creative and environmental groups that contribute in equal measure to the identity of the city. The Hotwells harbourside neighbourhood is home to the Create Centre, a major sustainability hub, and to Spike Island's artist community.

Away from the water, dramatic community-led rejuvenation is under way in St Pauls and Stokes Croft, with the Peoples Republic of Stokes Croft and many original Banksy works attracting widespread publicity. Hamilton House has become the nerve centre here for an army of local organisations, capturing the diversity and fervour of sustainable development in Bristol.

Harbourside round trip

The floating harbour is the lungs of Bristol. Set in the very middle of the city it provides both an open space to breathe and a transport route to many key venues. It defines the city's history as a one-time port and today its docksides are bustling with new businesses, restaurants, museums and homes. This circular tour starts at the Architecture Centre by Pero's footbridge and takes you along the water's edge, past the magnificent old industrial cranes to the ss Great Britain—an icon of Bristol's maritime past. It then leads you through this dockland area, which is home to Aardman and the Spike Island studios, to the river on the other side where the Create Centre houses numerous environmental organisations, exhibits and an eco-home.

Heading back again, the tour crosses to the other side of the harbour and passes by several good pubs, including the Grain Barge, a floating Bristol Beer Factory pub with local ales and a great view of the docks. The route continues eastwards along the water's edge to the new development around the Millennium Square, which includes a planetarium and science museum, and excellent, organic food at Bordeaux Quay restaurant and The Harbourside café bar.

This tour will take just over an hour to walk. If you have time to stop at all the places listed and choose to take a break it will take you a couple of hours, more if you stop for food and drink.

⇢ Where to start

The Architecture Centre is situated on the harbourside, next door to the YHA and Pero's Bridge. It is a 15-minute walk or five-minute cycle ride from Temple Meads station. There is very limited parking for cars in the city centre but plenty of bike stands.

For more travel information please refer to pp. 16–17.

Bordeaux Quay

1 The Architecture Centre

16 Narrow Quay, Bristol, BS1 4QA

Champions the creation of better quality neighbourhoods, buildings and public spaces.

See case study: 'Shaping buildings, shaping the future' on p. 124.

Turn left out of the Architecture Centre and follow the water's edge around the Arnolfini and over the swing bridge to the old industrial cranes beyond. Pass underneath the cranes and carry on down the harbourside, with the water on your right, all the way to the ss Great Britain, about ten minutes further on.

2 ss Great Britain

Great Western Dockyard, Gas Ferry Road, Bristol, BS1 6TY

The world's first iron-hulled, steam-powered ship.

See case study: 'A maritime Bristol icon' on p. 128.

Head up Gas Ferry Road leaving the harbour behind you. Coming out on Cumberland Road, turn right and the Spike Island artist studios and gallery are a hundred yards further on, in a pale red-brick building.

3 Spike Island

133 Cumberland Road, Bristol, BS1 6UX

Exhibition and studio space for artists and creative industries.

This former 1960s Brook Bond tea-packing factory has become a leading venue for the production and display of contemporary visual arts. The building is a hive of activity for painters, sculptors, printmakers, web designers, performance artists and more, all making the most of the studios, exhibition spaces and excellent café.

*Cross over Cumberland Road using the bridge and go down the first
set of steps to the path beside the river. Continuing in the same direction,
away from the harbour with the river on your left, follow the path all
the way along until it ends at the Create Centre, a huge red-brick building.*

4 Create Centre

Smeaton Road, Bristol, BS1 8XN

Vibrant environment centre hosting events, exhibitions and an eco-home.

See case study: 'An environmental hub' on p. 38.

*Retrace your steps a hundred yards or so to where the path meets
Cumberland Road. Passing though the gate, cross over to Avon Crescent
and head towards the bridge, passing the Nova Scotia pub. Just the other
side of the bridge turn right into the forecourt of the Pump House pub.
A walkway follows the harbourside from here, with the water on your right,
all the way to the Grain Barge about 15 minutes further on.*

5 The Grain Barge

Mardyke Wharf, Hotwells Road, Hotwells, Bristol, BS8 4RU

A friendly eating, drinking and music venue floating in the harbour.

Moored across from the ss Great Britain, this historic converted barge is
owned by the Bristol Beer Factory, an independent brewery that makes
award-winning ales. Much of the barge interior is made from reclaimed
and recycled materials. Fantastic fresh food is served upstairs and in the
evenings bands play in the bar below deck.

*Continue along the harbourside, in the same direction, keeping as close
to the water as you can. After 15 minutes or so you come to the
amphitheatre on a bend in front of the Lloyds building. Bordeaux Quay
restaurant is just around the corner, looking out over the water.*

6 Bordeaux Quay

V-Shed, Canons Way, Bristol, BS1 5UH

Independent restaurant committed to serving sustainable food.

An award-winning restaurant, deli, bakery, cookery school and bar,
Bordeaux Quay prides itself on sustainable food practices and
responsible energy use. Most ingredients are sourced from the West
Country, supporting local farmers and minimising food miles. It also runs
food education courses, teaching people the essential links between
good food, local produce and sustainability.

At Bristol is a large, glass-fronted building situated behind Bordeaux Quay on the edge of Millennium Square.

 At Bristol

Anchor Road, Harbourside, Bristol, BS1 5DB

One of the UK's largest interactive science centres.

This exhibition space engages the young and old in a gripping journey through science. With a planetarium and more than 300 interactive exhibits and displays, it offers both education and adventure. Grade II-listed, the building was originally a railway goods shed and has been updated with innovative energy-reduction features.

Coming out of At Bristol's main entrance, head across the small square towards Pero's Bridge. Don't cross the bridge but turn left and walk along the covered walkway by the water's edge. The Harbourside café bar is the last venue along this stretch, just past the Watershed media centre.

I♥ Bristol because...

there are so many, heroic cyclists, despite lots of traffic – more, more, more!

The Harbourside

Canons Road, The Harbourside, Bristol, BS1 5TX

Boathouse bistro and market space selling local produce.

Next door to the Watershed arthouse cinema, this old boathouse is a multi-use space housing a tapas bar, dining area, Victorian-style teashop, apothecary, flower shop and the Bristol Ferry Company ticket office. This is just what the waterfront needed, and it may expand into an outdoor food and craft market too.

The Harbourside is just two minutes from the start of the tour. You can catch a ferry from here to see the docks from the water or to return to Temple Meads station.

St Nicholas Market

Old town and new beginnings

The very old and very new sit cheek by jowl in Bristol's city centre. This tour takes in both, starting at the 900-year-old Temple Church and passing through the lovely old streets around the Corn Exchange before taking you to the grittier, more contemporary venues in Stokes Croft. There are places to pause for a picnic, such as Castle Park above the canal, or to have a snack or hearty meal, such as the numerous food stalls in St Nicholas Market. There is peace and calm in St Stephen's Church and advice on health and well-being at the Urban Fringe Dispensary along the way.

Leaving the older streets of downtown Bristol behind, the tour heads into a different slice of city life altogether. The vibe is palpable—a buzzy, fresh, creative counter culture, starting with the Jamaica Street Artist Studios and, beneath them, the office of the Peoples Republic of Stokes Croft. This is a Banksy endorsed zone, with graffiti on every spare wall and one of Banksy's own renowned murals at the entrance to Hamilton House— now a hub of social enterprises and the hip Canteen café bar. The tour finishes back in a more historic zone, in the Georgian grandeur of Portland Square.

This tour is best done on foot as it goes through places where bikes need to be pushed or even carried. It should take about an hour and a half to walk without stopping, but could easily last a half a day or more if you want to take it in more slowly.

 Where to start

Temple Church and Churchyard are in Church Lane, just off Victoria Street, a ten-minute walk or five-minute cycle ride from Temple Meads station. There is very limited street parking in the city centre with short-term meters in place.

For more travel information please refer to pp. 16–17.

1 Temple Church and Churchyard

Temple Street, off Victoria Street, Bristol, BS1 6DR

Knights Templar church dating back to the 12th century.

A listed building owned by English Heritage, this ruined church and its garden are a hidden jewel in the city centre. Bombed in the 1940 Bristol Blitz, it was left an empty shell. Only the foundations remain of the original, circular church; the walls that still stand are mostly 15th century.

Come out of Church Lane onto Victoria Street. Turn right and follow Victoria Street all the way along to the canal. Just over Bristol Bridge there is a path leading off right into Castle Park.

2 Castle Park

Bridge Road, Bristol, BS1 2AH

Newly developed park on an ancient riverside site.

A popular green space in the heart of Bristol, this park was created on the site of buildings bombed during the Second World War. Two ruined churches and the foundations of Bristol Castle can still be seen, alongside the herb garden, public artworks, a playground and seven trees commemorating the D-Day landings.

From the old church in the middle of the park walk out onto Newgate. Turn left and follow Newgate as it turns into Wine Street. As Wine Street bends round to the left keep going ahead into pedestrianised Corn Street. On Wednesdays this street is filled with the Farmers Market. St Nicholas Market is a covered area to the left of Corn Street, accessed via All Saints Lane.

③ St Nicholas Market

Corn Street, Bristol, BS1 1JQ

Home to the largest collection of independent retailers in Bristol.

Named as one of the ten best markets in the UK, St Nicholas has a wide array of clothes, crafts, flowers, jewellery and much more. The central aisle is lined with food stalls selling Italian, Portuguese, Caribbean and Moroccan dishes, as well as exotic juices, locally made bread and cheese, and Bristol's own Pieminister.

Head back out to Corn Street, turn left and walk a few blocks further towards the harbour. Where Corn Street turns into Clare Street there is a turning right into St Stephen's Street. The church and café are just down here on the left.

④ St Stephen's Church

21 St Stephens Street, Bristol, BS1 1EQ

A sacred, peaceful space with a café serving well-sourced food.

A Grade I-listed building developed in 1248 by Benedictines from Glastonbury Abbey, St Stephen's was rebuilt in 1470 and restored during the 19th century. It provides a Christian community presence in the city centre and explores faith through art, singing and dance.

Walk back out to Clare Street and turn right, continuing to the end. Cross over busy Colston Avenue to the area with the fountains. A Fair Cup is in the middle of this pedestrian zone.

⑤ A Fair Cup

Central Promenade, Bristol, BS1 4ST

Bristol-based company serving take-away fairtrade hot drinks.

This stall sells high quality, fairly traded tea, coffee and chocolate and offsets double its carbon emissions by investing in energy saving and renewable energy projects. A Fair Cup gives away its used coffee grounds as compost, and provides customers with blankets in winter (no need for outdoor gas heaters!).

Cross over the busy road on the other side of this pedestrian zone towards the Hippodrome theatre. Just to the right of the Hippodrome (as you face it) Colston Street leads off up the hill. Walk up Colston Street, past Colston Hall, and the Urban Fringe Dispensary is on your right, almost opposite the junction with Lower Park Row.

Did you know?

Urban dwellers generally moan about litter and refuse. But in Bristol just over half of respondents think that public spaces are kept well clear of rubbish.

6 Urban Fringe Dispensary

58 Colston Street, Bristol, BS1 5AZ

Traditional herbal apothecary providing medicines and advice.

This old-style apothecary provides herbal medicine, free over-the-counter advice, private consultations and a range of other complementary therapies from acupuncture to shiatsu. It runs courses on herbal medicine and is currently mapping the local area for herbs that can be foraged sustainably.

Continue up to the top of Colston Street and turn right onto Upper Maudlin Street. The Rag Trade Boutique is a little further on, on the right.

7 Rag Trade Boutique

2 Upper Maudlin Street, Bristol, BS2 8DJ

Buying, selling, trading pre-loved designer womenswear.

This is a funky clothes shop that recycles good-quality unwanted clothes. Bring in those dresses, shoes, accessories you don't wear anymore: RagTrade sells them on and gives you half the sale price—so you can buy something new! Anything unsold goes to charity, helping to reduce the 80% of UK clothes going to waste.

Cross over Upper Maudlin Street and continue down the road, passing the Bristol Royal Infirmary. Soon after the hospital turn left into Dighton Street, which turns into Jamaica Street. Just before the end there is a tall old building on the left, with red iron columns and large windows. Jamaica Street Artist studios are on the top three floors. Studios can be visited by appointment, or during the annual open studio weekend in June.

8 Jamaica Street Artists

39 Jamaica Street, Stokes Croft, Bristol, BS2 8JP

Thriving, ambitious collective of artist studios.

A Grade II-listed building and a landmark in Stokes Croft, this is one of the largest artist-led studios outside London, and home to 43 painters, sculptors and illustrators. Its open studio weekend every June is an unmissable opportunity to meet the artists, look at their exhibitions and buy affordable artworks.

Standing outside the Jamaica Street Artists building you will see Hamilton House across the main road in front of you. The Canteen café bar on the ground floor has a terrace along the pavement.

I♥ Bristol because...

you can randomly turn up and there is always something fun to see and do.

9 Coexist at Hamilton House

Hamilton House, 80 Stokes Croft, Bristol, BS1 3QY

Hub for a community of artists, musicians, charities and entrepreneurs.

See case study: 'At the cutting edge' on p. 125.

Turn left out of Hamilton House and follow Stokes Croft down nearly two blocks. Pieminister is on the left before the Full Moon pub.

Pieminister

24 Stokes Croft, Bristol, BS1 3PR

Award-winning pies handmade in Bristol.

A Bristol-based company set up in 2002, Pieminister provides the British public with sumptuous, handmade pies. All ingredients are locally sourced to make the ten standard pies and several extra seasonal ones. From the vegetarian Heidi to the beef- and chorizo-filled Matador, there's sure to be one that takes your fancy.

From Pieminister take the next left off Stokes Croft into Moon Street (by the pub) and then immediately right into Backfields. Turn right at the junction and immediately left into Wilder Street. From here, take the first right into Cave Street, which leads into Portland Square. The Pierian Centre is on the north side of the square.

11 The Pierian Centre

27 Portland Square, Bristol, BS2 8SA

Community Interest Company running a programme of community and arts events.

Based in a five-storey Georgian building, the Pierian Centre focuses on training and community development. Pierian means 'of knowledge' or 'of inspiration' in Greek and the centre aims to provide a calm space to encourage this. Its extensive range of courses and workshops includes drumming, Italian conversation, nutritional healing and advice on changing careers.

From Portland Square head back to Stokes Croft to catch a bus to the city centre or walk down to Bond Street to catch a bus to Temple Meads station.

Directory

 ## A Fair Cup

Central Promenade, Bristol, BS1 4ST
07779 014917
info@afaircup.com
www.afaircup.com

Bristol-based company serving take-away fairtrade hot drinks.

 ## African Initiatives

Brunswick Court, Brunswick Square, Bristol, BS2 8PE
0117 915 0001
info@african-initiatives.org.uk
www.african-initiatives.org.uk

Social justice organisation working with communities in Africa.

 ## The Architecture Centre

16 Narrow Quay, Bristol, BS1 4QA
0117 922 1540
info@architecturecentre.co.uk
www.architecturecentre.co.uk

Champions the creation of better quality buildings and public spaces.

See case study: 'Shaping buildings, shaping the future' on p. 124.

 ## ArtSpace LifeSpace at The Island

The Island, Silver Street, Bristol, BS1 2PY
0117 929 7534
info@artspacelifespace.com
www.theislandbristol.com

Multi-use arts complex in the heart of the city centre.

Located in an old fire station, this innovative venue houses a variety of creative spaces, from recording studios to public performance areas. It is managed by an artist-led workers cooperative, Artspace Lifespace, which enables the galleries and other facilities to be used by Bristol's wider creative community, including the renowned Invisible Circus.

Association of Sustainability Practitioners

C/o The Hub, Bush House, 72 Prince Street, Bristol, BS1 4QD
07795 632607
info@asp-online.org
www.asp-online.org

Connecting professionals around the world who share a belief in sustainable practice.

At Bristol

Anchor Road, Harbourside, Bristol, BS1 5DB
0845 3451235
information@at-bristol.org.uk
www.at-bristol.org.uk

One of the UK's largest interactive science centres.

Back To The Planet

Spike Island, 133 Cumberland Road, Bristol, BS1 6UX
0117 307 0779
info@backtotheplanet.co.uk
www.backtotheplanet.co.uk

Video production company with a big impact and a small footprint.

Back To The Planet is one of the UK's leading ethical video production companies. It works with organisations that recognise the impact that making their videos has on the environment, and it strives to make its own business operation as sustainable and ethically sound as possible.

 Bordeaux Quay

V-Shed, Canons Way, Bristol, BS1 5UH
0117 906 5550
info@bordeaux-quay.co.uk
www.bordeaux-quay.co.uk

Independent restaurant committed to serving sustainable food.

The Bristol Bike Project

Hamilton House, 80 Stokes Croft, Bristol, BS1 3QY
07516 320713
thebristolbikeproject@gmail.com
http://www.thebristolbikeproject.org

Community project doing up unwanted bikes for the underprivileged.

Bristol Credit Union

112 Cheltenham Road, Stokes Croft, Bristol, BS6 5RW
0117 924 7309
info@bristolcreditunion.org.uk
www.bristolcreditunion.org

Financial cooperative owned and controlled by its members.

 Bristol Farmers Market

Corn Street, Bristol, BS1 1JQ
0117 922 4014
markets@bristol.gov.uk
www.visitbristol.co.uk

Market selling local produce every Wednesday, 9.30am to 2.30pm.

Bristol Ferry Boat Company

M B Tempora, Welsh Back, Bristol, BS1 4SP
0117 927 3416
www.bristolferry.com

Public ferry services and private boat hire around the harbour and river.

Bristol Folk House

40a Park Street, Bristol, BS1 5JG
0117 926 2987
admin@bristolfolkhouse.co.uk
www.bristolfolkhouse.co.uk

Adult education centre, music venue and café selling organic, seasonal food.

 Bristol Natural History Consortium

3rd Floor, Bush House, 72 Prince Street, Bristol, BS1 4QD
0117 930 4926
info@bnhc.org.uk
www.bnhc.org.uk

Creating excellence in environmental communication through public and professional events.

 Bristol Wireless

Hamilton House, 80 Stokes Croft, Bristol, BS1 3QY
0117 325 0067
info@bristolwireless.net
www.bristolwireless.net

Social enterprise making connectivity, computers and free software available to all.

 Brunel's Buttery

Wapping Wharf, Bristol, BS1 6DS
0117 929 1696

Small shack serving hot drinks and bacon rolls—a Bristol institution.

 Business in the Community

Bush House, 72 Prince Street, Bristol, BS1 4QD
0117 930 9380
information@bitc.org.uk
www.bitc.org.uk

Works with businesses to improve their sustainability and ethical practice.

The Canteen

Hamilton House, 80 Stokes Croft, Bristol, BS1 3QY
0117 923 2017

Vibrant café bar with local food and drink on the menu.

 ## Castle Park

Bridge Road, Bristol, BS1 2AH
0117 922 3719
bristolparks@bristol.gov.uk

Newly developed park on an ancient riverside site.

 ## Coexist at Hamilton House

Hamilton House, 80 Stokes Croft, Bristol, BS1 3QY
0117 924 9599
info@coexistuk.org
www.coexistuk.org

Hub for a community of artists, musicians, charities and entrepreneurs.

See case study: 'At the cutting edge' on p. 125.

 ## The Converging World

3rd Floor, Bush House, 72 Prince Street, Bristol, BS1 4QD
0117 927 7089
info@theconvergingworld.org
www.theconvergingworld.org

Tackling climate change and poverty through linking world communities.

 ## The Cube Microplex Cinema

Dove Street South, Bristol, BS2 8JD
cubeadmin@cubecinema.com
http://microplex.cubecinema.com

Hosts a variety of entertaining activities, films, talks, gigs and shows.

 ## Ethical Property Company

Brunswick Square, St Pauls, Bristol, BS2 8PE
0117 916 6486
info@ethicalproperty.co.uk
www.ethicalproperty.co.uk

Develop property for charities, social enterprises and campaign groups.

Forum for the Future – Sustainable Bristol City Region

3rd Floor, Bush House, 72 Prince Street, Bristol, BS1 4QD
0117 930 7300
p.rainger@forumforthefuture.org
www.sustainablebristol.com

Ten-year programme to make Bristol the UK's most sustainable city region.

Full Moon Backpacker Hotel and Attic Bar

Stokes Croft, Bristol, BS1 3PR
0117 924 5007
info@fullmoonbristol.co.uk
www.fullmoonbristol.co.uk

Eco-friendly business offering accommodation, live music and organic food and drinks.

The Grain Barge

Mardyke Wharf, Hotwells Road, Hotwells, Bristol, BS8 4RU
0117 929 9347
gb@bristolbeerfactory.co.uk
www.grainbarge.com

Friendly eating, drinking and music venue floating in the harbour.

The Harbourside

1 Canons Road, The Harbourside, Bristol, BS1 5TX
0117 929 1100

Boathouse bistro and market space selling local produce.

The Hub

3rd Floor, Bush House, 72 Prince Street, Bristol, BS1 4QD
0117 370 0404
bristol.hosts@the-hub.net
www.bristol.the-hub.net

Shared office for people working to create a better world.

An inventive organisation that allows freelancers, small social enterprises and charities to hire office space and meeting rooms to suit their needs. This gives them the benefits of skills sharing, cheaper office rent and learning from each other. The Hub also puts on training sessions.

Imayla

4th Floor, Hamilton House, 80 Stokes Croft, Bristol, BS1 3QY
info@imayla.com
www.imayla.com

Education through participatory arts and environmental activities.

A not-for-profit company facilitating recreation and learning for young people, families and groups. Imayla co-ordinates residential learning experiences from dancing to mountain biking in rural settings. It promotes intercultural exchange and runs skills-based training.

Inspired Times Magazine

Unit 19, The Coach House, 2 Upper York Street, Bristol, BS2 8QN
0117 924 0901
sharon@inspiredtimesmagazine.com
www.inspiredtimesmagazine.com

National positive lifestyle magazine with an eye-catching design.

Jamaica Street Artists

39 Jamaica Street, Stokes Croft, Bristol, BS2 8JP
jsadevelopment09@yahoo.co.uk
http://jamaicastreetartists.co.uk

Thriving, ambitious collective of artist studios.

 Peoples Republic of Stokes Croft

PRSC Ground Floor, 37 Jamaica Street, Stokes Croft, Bristol, BS2 8JP
07866 627052
contact@prsc.org.uk
www.prsc.org.uk

Community Interest Company promoting the interests of Stokes Croft.

Campaigns against the historical neglect of this area by local government. It showcases the neighbourhood as a vibrant cultural quarter brimming with artistic, political and economic life. Stokes Croft is home to some of the city's best street art, which PRSC works to protect and maintain.

Pieminister

24 Stokes Croft, Bristol, BS1 3PR
0117 942 9372
stokescroft@pieminister.co.uk
www.pieminister.co.uk

Award-winning pies handmade in Bristol.

The Pierian Centre

27 Portland Square, Bristol, BS2 8SA
0117 924 4512
info@pieriancentre.com
www.pierian-centre.com

Community Interest Company running community and arts events.

 ## Potstop

42 The Grove, Bristol, BS1 4RB
0117 925 3403
potstop@hotmail.co.uk
www.fenwickdesign.co.uk/potstop

Pottery studio and workshop for ceramic courses.

 ## Quartet Community Foundation for the West of England

Royal Oak House, Royal Oak Avenue, Bristol, BS1 4GB
0117 989 7700
info@quartetcf.org.uk
www.quartetcf.org.uk

Community foundation helping donors support local causes and charities.

 ## Rag Trade Boutique

2 Upper Maudlin Street, Bristol, BS2 8DJ
0117 376 3085
info@ragtradeboutique.co.uk
www.ragtradeboutique.co.uk

Buying, selling, trading pre-loved designer womenswear.

 ## Rathbone Greenbank Investments

10 Queen Square, Bristol, BS1 4NT
0117 930 3000
greenbank@rathbones.com
www.rathbonegreenbank.com

Ethical investment service taking account of environmental and
social concerns.

The Schumacher Institute for Sustainable Systems

3rd Floor, Bush House, 72 Prince Street, Bristol, BS1 4QD
0117 927 3200
info@schumacherinstitue.org.uk
www.schumacherinstitute.org.uk

Research centre exploring sustainable social and environmental systems.

See case study: 'Pioneer environmentalists—the Schumacher story'
on p. 126.

 ## Slow Food Market

Corn Street, Bristol, BS1 1JQ
07976 072942
nick@slowfoodbristol.org
www.slowfoodbristol.org

Market selling local produce on the first Sunday of the month.

See case study: 'Food—local, tasty and slow' on p. 127.

 ## Soil Association

South Plaza, Marlborough Street, Bristol, BS1 3NX
0117 314 5000
info@soilassociation.org
www.soilassociation.org

UK's leading organic food and farming organisation.

The Soil Association promotes planet-friendly food through its certification scheme, campaigns, education programmes and community projects. It focuses on maintaining high organic standards while working to transform school food, develop its Land Trust project and raise awareness about the connection between healthy soil, healthy food and healthy people.

 ## The Spark

86 Colston Street, Bristol, BS1 5BB
0117 914 3434
editor@thespark.co.uk
www.thespark.co.uk

Regional magazine about positive change.

The UK's biggest ethical quarterly magazine, *The Spark* keeps people in touch with 'locally based creative solutions for a changing world'. It covers a huge range of topics from yoga to choirs to tea tasting. A fantastic free read that can be picked up in many venues in the South West.

 **Spike Island**

133 Cumberland Road, Bristol, BS1 6UX
0117 929 2266
admin@spikeisland.org.uk
www.spike-island.org.uk

Exhibition and studio space for artists and creative industries.

 ss Great Britain

Great Western Dockyard, Gas Ferry Road, Bristol, BS1 6TY
0117 926 0680
admin@ssgreatbritain.org
www.ssgreatbritain.org

The world's first iron-hulled, steam-powered ship.

See case study: 'A maritime Bristol icon' on p. 128.

 St Nicholas Market

Corn Street, Bristol, BS1 1JQ
www.stnicholasmarketbristol.co.uk

Home to the largest collection of independent retailers in Bristol.

 St Stephen's Church

21 St Stephens Street, Bristol, BS1 1EQ
0117 927 7977
info@saint-stephens.com

A sacred, peaceful space with a café serving well-sourced food.

 Streets Alive

86 Colston Street, Bristol, BS1 5BB
0117 922 5708
info@streetsalive.org.uk
www.streetsalive.org.uk

Organisation promoting neighbourhood street parties.

A not-for-profit group that promotes streets as social spaces. It provides training and advice to local authorities, neighbourhoods and businesses, and engages the public through activities concerning green travel, children's play and social cohesion.

Sustainability South West

Bush House, 72 Prince Street, Bristol, BS1 4QD
0117 929 0989
info@sustainabilitysouthwest.org.uk
www.sustainabilitysouthwest.org.uk

Charity that raises awareness and gives advice on action for sustainability.

2 Cathedral Square, College Green, Bristol, BS1 5DD
0117 926 8893
info@sustrans.org.uk
www.sustrans.org.uk

Leading UK charity for sustainable transport.

Sustrans promotes travel that benefits both our health and the environment. With its headquarters in Bristol, it works with communities and local authorities nationwide to change transport habits. A notable success is its National Cycle Network: 12,000 miles of cycle routes used by more than a million cyclists and walkers every day.

The 3rd Floor

Bush House, 72 Prince Street, Bristol, BS1 4QD
0117 929 9471
reception@the3rdfloor.org.uk
www.the3rdfloor.org.uk

Office space for organisations helping the transition to a new economy.

Tree Aid

Brunswick Court, Brunswick Square, Bristol, BS2 8PE
0117 909 6363
info@treeaid.org.uk
www.treeaid.org.uk

Helping communities in Africa's drylands fight poverty and improve the environment.

Urban Fringe Dispensary

58 Colston Street, Bristol, BS1 5AZ
0117 927 6527
info@urbanfringe.co.uk
www.urbanfringe.co.uk

Traditional herbal apothecary providing medicines and advice.

Vegetarian and Vegan Foundation

8 York Court, Wilder Street, Bristol, BS2 8QH
0117 970 5190
info@vegetarian.org.uk
www.vegetarian.org.uk

Monitors and explains scientific research linking diet to health.

 ## Volunteering Bristol

Royal Oak House, Royal Oak Avenue, Bristol, BS1 4GB
0117 989 7733
info@bristolvolunteers.org.uk
www.bristolvolunteers.org.uk

Promotes and develops opportunities for voluntary work.

 ## Wildscreen

Ground Floor, The Rackhay, Queen Charlotte Street, Bristol, BS1 4HJ
0117 328 5950
www.wildscreen.org.uk
info@wildscreen.org.uk

Charity promoting public appreciation of biodiversity through wildlife imagery.

See case study: 'Conservation through film' on p. 129.

 ## Zazu's Kitchen

45 Jamaica Street, Stokes Croft, Bristol, BS2 8JP
0117 923 2233
thecook@zazuskitchen.com
www.zazuskitchen.com

Upmarket café restaurant serving home-made food in casual, stylish setting.

The Architecture Centre

Shaping buildings, shaping the future

The Architecture Centre is the leading regional expert on engaging the public with the built environment and championing the creation of better quality neighbourhoods, buildings and public spaces. Based on Bristol's Harbourside, in the heart of the city, the Centre has an intimate and welcoming gallery, a resource room, a meeting room for hire, and a shop specialising in books on architecture and design as well as stylish, original gifts. The building is fully accessible and open every day of the week except Monday.

The Centre's programme includes exhibitions, events, lectures, debates, tours, walks and visits to inspiring buildings. It also provides built environment education and teaching resources to children and young people in the South West. The website provides further information on current activities: you can also sign up to the newsletter, or become a friend of the Architecture Centre.

Every aspect of the work undertaken here aims to develop appreciation of, and widen public awareness of, good architectural design. Everyone is affected by the public spaces around them. In every element of its programme, the Centre seeks to empower communities to shape their environment for the better. It also recognises the need to help the public understand what good architecture can offer them, and by finding innovative ways of presenting architecture it hopes to involve new audiences in an enthusiasm for great buildings and places. Through this it hopes to challenge preconceptions and stimulate greater demand for excellent architectural design.

Coexist at Hamilton House

At the cutting edge

Coexist is at the heart of the grassroots movement revitalising this area of Stokes Croft. Occupying a vast 1960s office block called Hamilton House, it has brought in numerous social enterprises, charities, musicians and artists, all with an interest in urban community projects and creating a more sustainable future. Set up in 2008, Coexist manages the space in the building to enable this wide range of Bristolians to develop their ideas alongside each other. Just a few years ago, Hamilton House was empty, its entrance an infamous haunt for street drinkers: now it is a dynamic community of 150 tenants, drawing people into Stokes Croft.

The network of people running Coexist have a holistic view of the needs of Hamilton House occupants. Taking into account transport requirements, energy use and the building's physical character their aim is to create a place in which innovation and creativity can flourish in a socially and ecologically sustainable environment. The idea for converting the building in this way was the brain-child of Coexist's directors, Oli Wells, Jamie Pike and Lizzie Keates, along with Martin Connolly and Eddie Callaghan (who own the building and, as benefactors, provided the seed funding for the project).

Work takes place in the upper floors of Hamilton House, but at ground level the spacious Canteen café bar provides Stokes Croft with a vibrant meeting place throughout the day and late into the night. The kitchen produces great food (with free soup and homemade bread for starters!), all seasonal, locally sourced and reasonably priced. The minimalist décor in the café is livened up with works by local artists, and at either end of the terrace—with its large flower beds growing herbs for the kitchen— are vast murals, including Banksy's famous Mild Mild West teddy bear throwing a petrol bomb.

The café bar is an enterprise involving further partners, including Jamie's brother Mat Pike and architect George Ferguson. Its success, and that of Coexist in general, in a run-down neighbourhood during a global recession, is remarkable and reflects the vision, belief and energy of all those individuals who dared to take the venture on.

The Schumacher Society

Pioneer environmentalists – the Schumacher story

The Schumacher Society was founded in 1978 following the death of environmental pioneer Fritz Schumacher. The core of the Society's work is its lecture series, which attracts inspirational speakers from across the world. The Society has also started other organisations: 20 years ago it formed the Schumacher College at Dartington in Devon, and in 2008 the Schumacher Institute for Sustainable Systems was founded in Bristol. The Institute is a research group that focuses on systems thinking for environmental and development issues at all scales, from local initiatives to global policy making. The various arms of the Institute encompass environmentalism, health, technologies, sustainability and education. Volunteers are always welcome to take part in its projects.

Addressing the need for psychological and spiritual well-being is also high on the agenda. Richard St George, who has been involved with the Schumacher Society from the beginning and was previously the UK director, says: 'If people aren't using their talents or communicating them, they may unconsciously compensate themselves with material rewards. This is substitution behaviour. We want to help people find their own path.' The Institute's Open Platform project was set up to nurture innovative ideas for sustainability and to mentor people in their efforts to find solutions to our overuse of the planet's resources. The 90-strong client base of Open Platform is supported by the Institute's comprehensive network of environmentalists, who give advice through regular evening seminars. Private mentoring sessions are also offered to help people build an effective career in sustainability.

The Society also publishes educational literature as the Schumacher Briefings. Plans for the future include a documentary outlining Fritz Schumacher's life and work to mark the centenary of his birth in 2011. The Society maintains close links with Schumacher College at Dartington, which provides a year-round programme of courses and lectures on subjects ranging from sustainable horticulture and renewable energy to holistic science and ecopsychology.

Slow Food Market

Food - local, tasty and slow

Slow Food Bristol began in 2004 as a local branch or 'convivium' of the international Slow Food movement. The Slow Food Market is one of its major successes and on the first Sunday of each month it fills Corn Street with the bright colours and fresh smells of good-quality local produce. Intended to complement rather than compete with the weekly Wednesday Farmers Market, the Slow Food Market champions producers of seasonal and sustainable food from the countryside surrounding Bristol.

The Slow Food group also organises themed meals, food and drink tastings, and visits to vineyards, farms and other markets in the region. It runs taste workshops, talks and cooking demonstrations. The group relishes high-quality, non-industrialised food—its texture, smell and taste—and in doing so strives to support the small-scale, independent growers and artisans who have maintained traditional production methods. As part of this campaign, Slow Food Bristol is developing initiatives to improve the standards of food in local schools: it helps to increase the amount of fresh food cooked on the premises, reduce food miles and provide a tastier, healthier alternative to the industrialised norm.

The summer of 2010 also saw the launch of the Urban Bee Project by Bristol Slow Food. This gives city dwellers the opportunity to take part in honey production based on traditional bee-keeping techniques—and to share in the delicious honey harvest! There are currently five enclosed hives in the Kingsdown area, with several more near the Downs and in Bishopston. Some people keep the bees, others help out by creating bee corridors. It's a project that could easily roll out across the whole of Bristol, building links within and across communities, teaching us more about plants and the role of bees, and giving us the chance to eat honey fresh from the hive.

ss Great Britain

A maritime Bristol icon

Designed by the legendary engineer Isambard Kingdom Brunel, the ss Great Britain is the world's first iron-hulled, steam-powered, ocean-going ship. At the time of her launch in 1843, she was the largest vessel in the world. The ship's curators preserve her as best they can and breathe new life into her history through interactive displays that allow people of all ages and abilities to enjoy and learn from their visits. Come at the right time and you might even catch a pianist playing old Victorian tunes on the lower deck.

At first glance, the ss Great Britain appears to be floating in the Avon River but closer inspection reveals a clever strategy to preserve the hull and enable visitors to explore beneath the surface. The ship actually sits in a dry dock, with a water-coated glass ceiling that creates this illusion of water. This has been necessary as corrosion has taken its toll on the ship after being exposed to salty sea water for so many years. Following the example of the US Air Force, which stores its aircraft in the Arizona desert, the curators preserve the ship's vast metal hull by replicating hot, dry conditions within the dock. This isn't easy in Bristol's cool, damp climate, especially while trying to reduce energy consumption. The solution begins with the air-cooling system in the dining saloon above the hull. Heat extracted from this system contributes to the process of creating dehumidified air to preserve the hull. Rather than drying the air throughout the dock, dehumidified air is pumped directly onto the metal. The water-coated ceiling acts as a blanket and provides sunlight and warmth for the ship and its visitors.

The ss Great Britain museum makes a concerted effort to save energy, minimise waste, and source local produce and services wherever possible. As an icon of Bristol, the ship is also very much part of its community. Local volunteers and Probation Service 'Pay Back Scheme' workers help the staff with the running of the ship. There are programmes with school groups and a Young Brunel scheme that encourages and supports budding young engineers. The new Brunel Institute provides learning facilities and free access to the library and archives of one of the most significant maritime collections in the UK.

Wildscreen

Conservation through film

Wildscreen is a charity promoting conservation through wildlife imagery. Part of the Bristol-based Natural History Consortium, its has grown to have a global reach over the past 25 years. Its main aim is to enthuse, educate and inspire people around the world to document and conserve species. One of its key initiatives is ARKive, a project to create an online archive of wildlife footage and photographs to facilitate learning about plants, animals and fungi. This has produced a large and informative catalogue of species that provides general facts and related media content—an excellent educational tool.

For the Year of Biodiversity in 2010, ARKive has gathered media content for 17,000 of the world's most endangered species. Anyone can get involved in this project and become a 'media donor' by contributing footage and photos. If you have expert knowledge of certain species and their habitats you can also help by authenticating the existing profiles. There are currently 6,000 species catalogued online with more than 40,000 associated video clips and photographs. The sharing and contribution of this media content is facilitated by ARKive's online social media presence: you can easily upload videos and photos to sites such as Facebook, YouTube, Flickr and Twitter.

Another of Wildscreen's hugely successful initiatives is the Wildscreen Film Festival, which takes place every other year in October. The event's Panda Awards recognise the best documentation of wildlife and the natural environment by film-makers across the world. There is always work for volunteers at the festival if you want to take part. Wildscreen plays a crucial role through these projects in educating the public about our biologically diverse world, and thereby helping to prevent the extinction of our most endangered species.

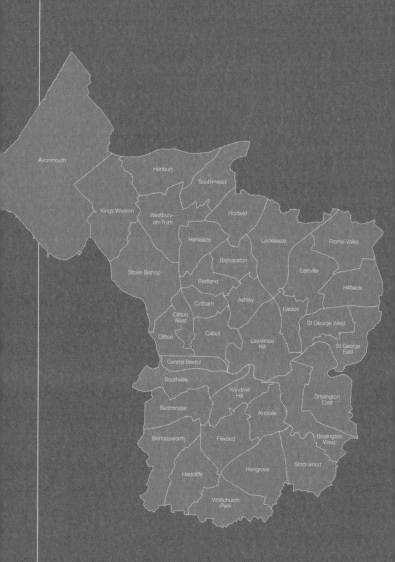

Avonmouth

Henbury

Southmead

Kings Weston

Westbury-
on-Trym

Horfield

Lockleaze

Frome Valley

Henleaze

Bishopston

Eastville

Hillfields

Stoke Bishop

Redland

Ashley

Easton

St George West

Cotham

Clifton
West

Cabot

Lawrence
Hill

St George
East

Clifton

Central Bristol

Southville

Windmill
Hill

Brislington
East

Bedminster

Knowle

Brislington
West

Bishopsworth

Filwood

Stockwood

Hartcliffe

Hengrove

Whitchurch
Park

Citywide

In every city people cross over neighbourhood boundaries with their activities and thinking. This is the case with many of the entries in this guidebook: groups, organisations and businesses working in certain areas of Bristol share their knowledge and skills with others beyond.

This Citywide section takes the non-local criteria a step further. It provides a platform for ideas, projects and groups that were initially created with a citywide remit, or have become more city focused over the years. These are virtual places that are not rooted in specific locations but are well worth knowing about. They cover a wide range of interests from food, energy and transport to community groups, media and trading. They also include the Bristol Green Capital Initiative, which has supported the idea of this good living guidebook.

STOKES CROFT BULLETIN

Directory

 ## Barter Buddies

86 Bower Road, Ashton, Bristol, BS3 2LU
info@barterbuddies.co.uk
www.barterbuddies.co.uk

Enables like-minded people to exchange goods and services.

 ## Better by Bike

www.betterbybike.info

Provides cycling information for Bristol and the surrounding area.

Bristol is the UK's first cycling city. The Better by Bike website helps to get you on your bike and start exploring the local area. Whether you want to start cycling for the first time, join a cycling club or need maps and routes, all the information can be found here.

 ## Bread Youth Project

The Proving House, 21 Sevier Street, St Werburghs, Bristol, BS2 9LB
info@breadyouthproject.org.uk
www.breadyp.org.uk

Social education to build up young people's skills and confidence.

 ## Bristol Civic Society

01454 632265
www.bristolcivicsociety.org.uk

Improves Bristol's built environment and celebrates its heritage.

An independent, voluntary organisation, the Civic Society has existed since 1905. It protects Bristol's built environment and heritage by influencing major new developments and monitoring planning applications. With more than 400 members, it puts on a varied events programme and publishes a newsletter and e-bulletin.

St Nicholas Market

 ## Bristol Cycle Campaign

info@bristolcyclingcampaign.org.uk
www.bristolcyclingcampaign.org.uk

Promotes cycling in Bristol through campaigns and social events for cyclists.

 ## Bristol Festival of Ideas

Leigh Court, Abbots Leigh, Bristol, BS8 3RA
ideas@gwebusinesswest.co.uk
www.ideasfestival.co.uk

Promotes discussion and debate with events throughout the year.

 ## Bristol Green Capital Initiative

green.capital@bristol.gov.uk
www.bristolgreencapital.org

Bringing communities together to make Bristol a green city.

 ## Bristol Green Doors Community Interest Company

info@bristolgreendoors.org
www.bristolgreendoors.org

Encouraging energy efficiency in homes through open doors events.

Bristol Green Doors opened more than 50 energy smart homes to the public in September 2010. The properties displayed a range of energy-efficiency improvements, from low-cost insulation to solar PV panels and rainwater harvesting. Follow-up workshops provided advice on improving your own home.

Bristol Health Trainers

07973 116231
mandyshute@nhs.net
www.bristolhealthtrainers.co.uk

Encourages and supports adults to develop a healthier lifestyle.

I ♥ Bristol because...

you can have a swim in the Clifton Lido, visit Jamaica Street Open Studios and see a naked bike ride all before lunch. Wonderful!

 Bristol Indymedia

bristol@indymedia.org
www.bristol.indymedia.org

Volunteer-run, open-access, user-generated news and events website.

 Bristol Local Food

10-12 Picton Street, Montpelier, Bristol, BS6 5QA
info@bristolfoe.org.uk
www.bristollocalfood.co.uk

Directory for locally produced food, recommended by local people.

Bristol Friends of the Earth (BFoE) produces this local food directory, which tells you where to find your favourite fruit and vegetables. You can also enter your own information on where to buy food. The BFoE local food news update is well worth subscribing to.

 Bristol Permaculture Group

07765 604571
bristol_permaculture@yahoo.co.uk

Runs community orchards, allotments, school gardens and skills-sharing courses.

City Car Club

0845 3301234
bristol@citycarclub.co.uk
www.citycarclub.co.uk

Pay-as-you-go car hire: hassle-free, environmentally friendly motoring.

 Ecojam

admin@ecojam.org
www.ecojam.org

Online guide to Bristol's local, green and ethical scene.

A very useful guide to the hot topics, products and events that Bristol greenies are involved in. Its weekly bulletin for subscribers is a great round-up of recent happenings. The directory, jobs and free stuff on the site are also worth a look.

 Environmental Research Web

IOP Publishing, Dirac House, Temple Back, Bristol, BS1 6BE
0117 929 7481
info@environmentalresearchweb.org
http://environmentalresearchweb.org

Website providing analysis and commentary on all areas of environmental research.

 The Freeconomy Community

Radford Mill Farm, Timsbury, Bath, BA2 0QF
mark@justfortheloveofit.org
www.justfortheloveofit.org

Builds resilient communities through sharing skills, tools and knowledge.

 Freecycle Bristol

http://groups.yahoo.com/group/FreecycleBristol

Online network for giving away and receiving things for free.

Freecycle is an expanding, worldwide, grassroots movement of people who give away things they don't need and acquire for free things they do need. Made up of individual groups across the globe, volunteer moderators run each local network.

Happy City Initiative

07836 706978
info@happycity.org.uk
www.happycity.org.uk

Enables communities to increase happiness through collaboration
and celebration.

This initiative inspires and enables Bristolians to spread greater happiness
and well-being by making more of their streets and neighbourhoods. It
connects people whose ideas and energy contribute to this goal. The
website includes inspiring quotes, pledges, events listings and ideas from
other successful happiness projects.

 Low Carbon South West

The Innovation Centre, Broad Quay, Bath, BA1 1UD
s.a.bond@bath.ac.uk
www.lowcarbonsouthwest.co.uk

Association incorporating the Bristol Environmental Technologies and
Services group.

This trade association brings together businesses, academics, investors,
local authorities and regional and national agencies to promote the growth
of the environmental technologies and services sector in Bristol, Bath and
the South West. Formerly in Bristol it is now based in Bath.

 Neighbourhood Partnerships

http://bristolpartnership.org/neighbourhood-partnerships

Give communities a greater say in local issues and services,

There are 14 neighbourhood partnerships across Bristol, managed by the
City Council with partner agencies such as Avon and Somerset Police and
Avon Primary Care Trust. The partnerships provide communities with an
opportunity to become more involved in the management of their
local services.

 North South Forum

Oxfam South West Campaigns, Brunswick Court, Brunswick Square,
Bristol, BS2 8PE
0117 916 6473
rjames@oxfam.org.uk
www.digitalbristol.org/members/nsf

Collective of non-profit organisations collaborating on sustainable
development issues.

Selfsufficientish

www.selfsufficientish.com

Website stuffed full of advice and information on how to be self-sufficient.

 Shift Bristol Community Interest Company

shiftbristol@yahoo.co.uk
www.shiftbristol.org.uk

Providing holistic, solution-based, practical learning to prepare for a low carbon future.

 The Source Magazine

Watercress Farm, Upton Lane, Dundry, Bristol, BS41 8NS
editor@thesource-southwest.co.uk
www.thesource-southwest.co.uk

Quarterly publication celebrating the best of sustainable living in the South West.

 Stop Bristol Airport Expansion Ltd

The Hub Bristol, 3rd Floor, Bush House, 72 Prince Street,
Bristol, BS1 4QD
email@stopbia.com
www.stopbia.com

Fighting the unsustainable expansion of Bristol Airport and its impact.

 Transition Bristol

C/o Phillip Corbin and Associates, Trym Lodge, 1 Henbury Road,
Westbury-on-Trym, Bristol, BS9 3HQ
0117 963 8323
team@transitionbristol.net
www.transitionbristol.net

Community-led response to climate change and peak oil.

 Transport for Greater Bristol Alliance

C/o 86 Colston Street, Bristol, BS1 5BB
info@tfgb.org.uk
www.tfgb.org.uk

Campaign to reduce congestion and provide better public transport.

Avonmouth

Henbury

Southmead

Kings Weston

Westbury-
on-Trym

North End

Kings Weston House and Blaise Castle Estate, two impressive stately homes, are the best-known landmarks in this part of town. Beyond these, North End is little explored by outsiders, but at least fifty thousand people live here in Avonmouth, Lawrence Weston, Shirehampton, Sea Mills, Westbury-on-Trym, Coombe Dingle, Henbury and Southmead.

The area has been quietly going about its business for decades, with little change to its numbers or ethnic make-up. The swarms of children running around Southmead's 50-year-old adventure playground are balanced out by the large proportion of pensioners walking to the shops and clipping their garden hedges. Maybe the wide array of open spaces on the doorstep makes North End quieter than elsewhere, as human impact is soaked up in local nature reserves such as Badock's Wood.

Lift the lid just a little, however, and you can see new activity emerging. In neighbourhoods that often find it hard to make ends meet, local groups are taking the initiative to form support networks like the Barrowmead Project. Others are fostering community links through places such as the Lawrence Weston Community Farm and Avonmouth Community Centre. In Westbury-on-Trym the local Transition group is mustering the masses through a new annual EcoFiesta. The 'Proud To Be A Meader' project and the Juicy Blitz youth juice bar on Lawrence Weston Parade are also bringing pride back to the area, and putting well-being and good living back on the agenda. As elsewhere in the city, change is taking place in the most northern reaches of Bristol.

Kings Weston House

Northern stretch explore

This tour travels out to the most northern point of Bristol, following the river to the port at Avonmouth before heading back to the farms and gardens of Lawrence Weston. It starts at Sea Mills train station, which has a stunning view of the River Avon with the Suspension Bridge hanging across the gorge. It then follows traffic-free cycle routes all the way to Avonmouth where the vibrant community centre and garden give you a feel for the neighbourhood. The windmills here indicate the port's progress towards becoming the South West's renewable energy hub.

Cycling back towards Lawrence Weston you come to one of Bristol's wonderful community farms. Enjoy a break on a picnic bench while watching the pigs, goats and geese, or take a stroll along the farm's new woodland walk. This is followed by the magnificent Kings Weston House, a beautiful Georgian mansion with expansive gardens hidden from the main road. Its underground tea room will provide sustenance before you head off to the Kingsweston Stables, where the setting alone is worth a visit—a real countryside feel within the city limits. If you want to do some horse riding phone ahead to get a pony saddled up ready for your arrival.

To cycle this tour gently with stop-offs will take a couple of hours. To walk around is equally possible as a morning or afternoon trip.

 **Where to start**

Sea Mills station is a 25-minute train ride from Bristol Temple Meads. It can also be reached by bike along the A4 Portway traffic-free link from central Bristol. There is limited car parking here.

For more travel information please refer to pp. 16–17.

View from Sea Mills station

1 Sea Mills train station

Sea Mills, Bristol, BS9 1SU

A stop on the Severn Beach line linking the city centre and industrial port.

This station was built in 1865 and became part of the Severn Beach line in 1922. It has a good regular service and is an important transport link for people living in this area of Bristol and for workers in Avonmouth.

From Sea Mills train station join the traffic-free route along the left-hand side of the Portway and follow it until you come to a crossing that takes you onto Park Road. Follow this road as it turns into Shirehampton High Street, bearing left. Continue on as this becomes Lower High Street. As you approach the bridge for the M5 look out for Sustrans Route 41 signs. Turn right onto Route 41 to follow part of the Avon Cycleway (an 85-mile route around Bristol). Follow this route until you near Lawrence Weston Community Farm (at this point you may want to stop at the farm but we'd encourage you to travel on to Avonmouth).

Follow Route 41 past the farm as it joins Lawrence Weston Road. Go to the end of the road and take a left at the roundabout to reach Kings Weston Lane. Turn right and follow the road to the end (passing under the motorway). Turn left onto St Andrews Road and at the end of this stretch go over the roundabout onto McClaren Road. As you reach Avonmouth Road turn left to arrive at Avonmouth Community Centre on your right.

② Avonmouth Community Centre

257 Avonmouth Road, Bristol, BS11 9EN

Hosts many activities and contains a garden, sports area and Avonmouth library.

See case study: 'Energy on the Bristol Channel' on p. 155.

Retrace your steps back to Lawrence Weston Community Farm to return to the rest of this tour.

③ Lawrence Weston Community Farm

Saltmarsh Drive, Bristol, BS11 0NJ

Community-run farm working to improve local quality of life.

See case study: 'Learning and inclusion down on the farm' on p. 157.

From the farm take the path that links you back into the housing estate at Saltmarsh Drive. Turn right here to join Long Cross. At the junction turn right and at the roundabout turn left onto Kings Weston Lane. Follow the lane until you come to Kings Weston House on the right-hand side.

North End fact :

Having wide-open, well-maintained spaces to enjoy, such as Blaise Castle Estate, is really appreciated in Westbury-on-Trym, where 93% of respondents are happy walkers.

④ Kings Weston House

Kings Weston Lane, Bristol, BS11 0UR

A fabulous Georgian mansion with an underground tea room.

Set in 28 acres of parkland the house was built in the early 1700s and has a lively history. Since 2000 it has been used as a venue for business and private events. With its grand entrance and views over the Bristol Channel, it is popular for civil ceremonies and for filming.

Come out of the main exit on Kings Weston Lane and cross over into Napier Miles Road. Turn left at the end onto Kings Weston Road. The stables are a few hundred metres further up on the right-hand side (please book ahead for a riding lesson or hack).

I ♥ Bristol because...

it's the smallest big city in England.

 Kingsweston Stables

Kings Weston Road, Lawrence Weston, Bristol, BS11 0UX

Riding school for all abilities in a stunning setting.

There are more than 20 horses in this riding school, set in beautiful wooded countryside within striking distance of the city centre. The stables are open from Wednesday to Sunday and offer group and private classes, with escorted hacking and pony riding for small children.

Now at the end of the tour you can either return to Sea Mills train station via Kings Weston Road and back along the Portway, or you can catch a bus back into town from Kings Weston Road.

Northern family ramble

Blaise Castle Estate is one of the gems of northern Bristol. A 650-acre, Grade II-listed parkland with deep wooded limestone gorges, open hill tops and a folly castle, the estate is an adventure in itself. The tour starts on the northern side of Blaise and takes you right through the park, past Goram's Chair and Coombe Farm, and out into Westbury-on-Trym. Here in the village you can stock up on fruit and other supplies at James the Greengrocer—a delightful fruit and veg shop set up by the youngest greengrocer ever. From Westbury-on-Trym the tour leads you towards Southmead and the wildlife haven of Badock's Wood. Just beyond the wood is the Adventure Playground, one of Bristol's oldest playgrounds but still much-loved by the children racing around there today.

Taking little legs as well as long ones into consideration, this tour could take a couple of hours to walk or, with stops along the way, most of a day. If you want to cycle around be aware that cycling is only allowed on parts of the route.

 **Where to start**

Blaise Castle Estate is accessed from Kings Weston Road on the B4057. There are frequent bus services to the estate as well as a large car park with dedicated disabled spaces.

For more travel information please refer to pp. 16–17.

I♥ Bristol because...

nature seems to fill every nook and cranny.

1 Blaise Castle Estate

Kings Weston Road, Lawrence Weston, Bristol, BS10 7QS

Magnificent Grade II-listed house and extensive wooded parkland.

See case study: 'Giants, castles and adventure' on p. 156.

From the main house follow the route through the estate that takes you past Goram's Chair and Coombe Farm (with a little detour to the castle folly to see some impressive views) until you reach an exit via The Dingle onto Canford Lane. Turn left and follow the road until you draw level with the entrance to Canford Cemetery. Cross the road and enter the cemetery. Pass through the rows of gravestones until you come to an exit by a large football field. Follow the path around this field until you reach Red House Lane. Carry on until this road, turning into Stoke Grove, meets Stoke Lane. Turn left here and follow the road until you come to James the Greengrocer at number 123.

I♥ Bristol because...

moving here was the best move of my life.

2 James the Greengrocer

123 Stoke Lane, Westbury-on-Trym, Bristol, BS9 3RW

Independent store that puts together fruit and veg boxes for collection.

In 2009, aged 19, James decided to set up a greengrocers rather than study for a law degree. His store has a welcoming, farmhouse feel, with fruit and veg laid-out in wicker baskets and wooden boxes. He supplies local pubs and restaurants, and is planning to source produce from allotment holders.

From James' carry on along Stoke Lane and cross over Falcondale Road to end up in the centre of Westbury-on-Trym village. There are a number of lovely shops and cafés here to stop for refreshments. From the main roundabout in the village turn into Westbury Hill and take the first left onto Water's Lane. At the next junction turn slightly left onto Eastfield Road and continue until a roundabout, where you turn left into Lake Road. Take the first left again onto Lakewood Road to access Badock's Wood.

3 Friends of Badock's Wood

Entrance: on Lakewood Road, Southmead, Bristol, BS10

Group that cares for this tucked-away broadleaf woodland.

In conjunction with the City Council, the friends group protects this ten-acre wildlife haven and develops its educational facilities. Designated a Local Nature Reserve in 2008, the wood has a Bronze Age burial mound and the River Trym running through its limestone valley.

Walk through the wood in an easterly direction, following the path through Bowness Gardens, until you come out onto Doncaster Road. Turn right and the Southmead Adventure Playground is just ahead of you.

Southmead Adventure Playground

Doncaster Road, Bristol, BS10 5PP

Much-loved, long-standing play area for under-14s.

Opened in 1955, the oldest adventure playground in Bristol is still going strong. Outside is a large run-a-round structure, aerial runway and American swing, with an under-8s play area nearby; indoors there is a soft play area and a craft room. Off-site activities include residentials in the Wye Valley.

If you want to remain in a more serene setting walk on through Doncaster Road Park and follow the River Trym out to finish at Shetland Road. Walk up Doncaster Road or Shetland Road to Southmead Road to catch frequent buses towards Filton or the city centre. Alternatively, cycle from here back towards town over the Downs and through Clifton.

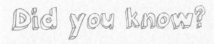

Natural resources, like parks and rivers, are highly prized by Bristolians. But only half of those responding to this survey are happy with the state of those in their neighbourhood.

Directory

 ## Atwood Drive Allotment Association

Lawrence Weston Road, Lawrence Weston, Bristol, BS11 0ST
0117 922 3737
mikesmith688@aol.com
www.webjam.com/atwood_drive_allotment

Hosts a community of people growing their own fruit and veg.

 ## Avonmouth Children's Centre

Avonmouth Primary School, Catherine Street, Avonmouth,
Bristol, BS11 9LG
0117 903 0271
avonmouth.cc@bristol.gov.uk

Parent and family support team with a crèche and meeting room.

 ## Avonmouth Community Centre

257 Avonmouth Road, Bristol, BS11 9EN
0117 982 7445
info@avonmouthcca.org.uk
www.avonmouthcca.org.uk

Hosts many activities and contains a garden, sports area and
Avonmouth library.

See case study: 'Energy on the Bristol Channel' on p. 155.

 ## Barrowmead Project Ltd

117-119 Longcross, Lawrence Weston, Bristol, BS11 0LP
0117 373 0267
ashley@barrowmead.co.uk
www.barrowmead.co.uk

Community endeavour to improve living standards in Lawrence Weston.

The Greenway Centre

Three local groups, Lawrence Weston Drugs and Alcohol Project, Severn Four Credit Union and Action on Health, joined together in the 1990s to create this community resource centre and healthy living programme. Activities include a freewheelers cycling group, the lean-and-green gardening group, and a befriending scheme for older people.

 ## Blaise Castle Estate

Kings Weston Road, Lawrence Weston, Bristol, BS10 7QS
0117 353 2266
blaise.estate@bristol.gov.uk
www.bristol.gov.uk/blaisecastleestate

Magnificent Grade II-listed house and extensive wooded parkland.

See case study: 'Giants, castles and adventure' on p. 156.

 ## Charity Search

25 Portview Road, Avonmouth, Bristol, BS11 9LD
0117 982 4060
info@charitysearch.org.uk
www.charitysearch.org.uk

Links elderly people in financial difficulty with established charities.

 ## Friends of Badock's Wood

Entrance: on Lakewood Road, Southmead, Bristol, BS10
0117 922 3719
badockswood@tiscali.co.uk
www.fobw.org.uk

Group that cares for this tucked-away broadleaf woodland.

The Greenway Centre

Doncaster Road, Bristol, BS10 5PY
0117 950 3335
reception@greenwaycentre.com
www.greenwaycentre.com

Home of the Southmead Development Trust, and heart of the
Southmead community.

 ## The Inner Heart

Imperial Chambers, Gloucester Road, Avonmouth, BS11 9AQ
0117 982 4793
contact@theinnerheart.co.uk
www.theinnerheart.co.uk

Services and treatments to promote well-being, health and harmony.

 ## James the Greengrocer

123 Stoke Lane, Westbury-on-Trym, Bristol, BS9 3RW
0117 962 3074

Independent store that puts together fruit and veg boxes for collection.

 ## Juicy Blitz

70 Ridingleaze, Lawrence Weston, Bristol, BS11
0117 982 4963
emma@breadyouthproject.org.uk
www.breadyp.org.uk/juicyblitz.asp

Juice and smoothie bar refurbished and developed by and for teenagers.

 ## Kings Weston House

Kings Weston Lane, Bristol, BS11 0UR
0117 938 2299
enquiries@kingswestonhouse.co.uk
www.kingswestonhouse.co.uk

Fabulous Georgian mansion with an underground tea room.

 ## Kingsweston Stables

Kings Weston Road, Lawrence Weston, Bristol, BS11 0UX
0117 982 8929
www.kingswestonstables.com

Riding school for all abilities in a stunning setting.

Lawrence Weston Community Farm

Saltmarsh Drive, Bristol, BS11 0NJ
0117 938 1128
office@lwfarm.org.uk
www.lwfarm.org.uk

Community-run farm working to improve local quality of life.

See case study: 'Learning and inclusion down on the farm' on p. 157.

 ## Lawrence Weston Community Transport

117-119 Long Cross, Bristol, BS11 0LP
0117 907 3074
lwct.bristol@talk21.com

Non-profit organisation helping people with mobility problems.

This growing community project is run by local people and currently owns four minibuses. It operates several transport schemes for residents of Lawrence Weston and the surrounding areas. The Link Service operates Monday to Friday and vehicles can be hired by groups with a driver.

 ## Natural England (Southwest stewardship)

Block 3 Government Buildings, Burghill Road, Westbury-on-Trym, Bristol, BS10 6NJ
0845 6024098
westofengland@naturalengland.org.uk
www.naturalengland.org.uk
Provides advice on how best to safeguard England's natural wealth.

 ## New Brunswick United Reformed Church

Wigton Crescent, Southmead, Bristol, BS10 6DY
0117 950 7776
newbrunswickurc@hotmail.co.uk
www.redlandparkchurch.co.uk

Small church hosting a variety of community events.

 ## Proud To Be A Meader

Southmead Youth Centre, Greystoke Avenue, Bristol, BS10 6AS
0117 377 3605
marie.stoner@bristol.gov.uk
www.proud2bameader.com

Community involvement in positive developments in Southmead.

The Rock Community Centre

St Peters Hall, Ridingleaze, Bristol, BS11 0QE
0117 938 4636
rock@lawrenceweston.fsnet.co.uk
www.therockcommunitycentre.com

Community facility for local people, especially the elderly and disabled.

 ## Sea Mills train station

Sea Mills, Bristol, BS9 1SU

A stop on the Severn Beach line linking the city centre and industrial port.

 ## Shirehampton Community Action Forum

Shirehampton Public Hall, 32 Station Road, Bristol, BS11 9TX
0117 982 9963
ash@shirecaf.org.uk
www.shirecaf.org.uk

Grassroots development organisation working with young people, environment and planning.

 ## Shirehampton Public Hall

32 Station Road, Shirehampton, Bristol, BS11 9TX
0117 982 9963
bookings@shirepubhall.org.uk
http://hall.shire.org.uk

Provides leisure and educational facilities for all ages in the community.

 ## Southmead Adventure Playground

Doncaster Road, Bristol, BS10 5PP
0117 950 3607
southmead.apg@bristol.gov.uk
www.goplacestoplay.org.uk

Much-loved, long-standing play area for under-14s.

Southmead Community Centre

Southmead Community Association, Greystoke Avenue,
Bristol, BS10 6AS
0117 950 1187
info@southmeadcommunitycentre.org.uk
www.southmeadcommunitycentre.org.uk

Runs family nights, dance classes, coffee mornings and more.

 # Southmead Community Sport

Pen Park Sports Pavillion, Jarratts Road, Southmead,
Bristol, BS10 6WF
0117 950 8362
southmeadcommunitysport@hotmail.com
www.southmeadcommunitysport.co.uk

Sports club run by local volunteers.

 # Southmead Contact and Resource Team (SCART)

169 Greystoke Avenue, Bristol, BS10 6AS
0117 950 2000
karen.tg@virgin.net

A one-stop shop for advice and information for local residents.

 # Southmead Development Trust

Greenway Centre, Doncaster Road, Southmead, Bristol, BS10 5PY
0117 950 3335
information@southmead.org
www.southmead.org

Develops opportunities for growth in the local community.

See case study: 'Business alongside well-being' on p. 158.

 # Southmead Pride

175 Greystoke Avenue, Southmead, Bristol, BS10 6BA
0117 959 3999
cliffsflorists@btconnect.com
www.southmeadpride.co.uk

Website advertising events and clubs, including the Christmas
Bus appeal.

Southmead Youth Centre

Greystoke Avenue, Bristol, BS10 6AS

0117 377 3605

marie.stoner@bristol.gov.uk

Offers a range of activities and information for 10- to 19-year-olds.

 Sustainable Westbury-on-Trym (SusWot)

Meetings held at: Westbury-on-Trym Primary School, Channell's Hill, Bristol, BS9 3HZ

0117 950 4238

suswot2050@gmail.com

www.suswot.org.uk

Local group working to create a happier, more sustainable, closer-knit community.

See case study: 'Using less, living more' on p. 159.

 Westbury-on-Trym Farmers Market

Westbury Hill Car Park, Westbury Hill, Westbury-on-Trym, Bristol, BS9 3AG

Local produce market on the fourth Saturday of each month.

 Westbury-on-Trym Society (WOTSOC)

0117 950 6807

info@westburyontrymsociety.org.uk

www.westburyontrymsociety.org.uk

Well established society maintaining the village's attractive environment.

 Working in Southmead for Health (WISH)

Badocks Wood Primary School, Room 31, Doncaster Road, Southmead, Bristol, BS10 5PU

0117 903 1623

karen.tg@virgin.net

www.bristol.gov.uk

Runs a play scheme, activities for older people and a domestic abuse forum.

Avonmouth Community Centre

Energy on the Bristol Channel

Avonmouth Community Centre (ACC) uses a ship in its logo to represent the strong bond between this neighbourhood and the sea. Sitting on the edge of the Bristol Channel, Avonmouth village has long been surrounded by the cargo ships and heavy industry of Bristol's port. Today, many residents are excited about the wind turbines being erected along the shoreline near their homes. Surrounded by the history of the docks, Avonmouth is now mooted to become the South West's renewable energy hub in the near future.

The art group of the ACC has further highlighted the neighbourhood's connection with the sea by donating maritime oil paintings to line the centre's walls. This is just one of many activities taking place here that bring local people together to enjoy each other's company. One ACC regular says, 'The centre is part of the community. I don't have to travel far to meet people I wouldn't meet otherwise.' There has been such a growth of activities and local involvement recently that for the first time the centre's trustees have appointed a manager, Alv Hirst, to provide some guidance and to move things on. The centre now has a number of groups that use the facilities, including NHS Health Trainers, two youth groups (one called Avon Loud Mouth!) and a youth theatre.

Alv thinks that two improvements at the centre have helped this upturn in interest: the newly fitted kitchen and the landscaped garden at the rear. Both have shown people that the space is user-friendly and accessible. The garden has easy wheelchair access and raised beds filled with sensory plants such as lavender and fennel. 'For me, it means a place where I can relax,' one visitor says. Projects for the future include a youth gardening group and a food-buying group to complement the need for better access to healthy food choices, training and socialising.

ACC seems to have caught a mood in Avonmouth, as in other parts of Bristol, for people wanting to work together to improve their local environment. As Alv says, 'Avonmouth village is a hidden gem. The community has people with amazing energy, fascinating history and great ideas.

Blaise Castle Estate

Giants, castles and adventure

Blaise Castle Estate, situated on the high ground of northern Bristol, is filled with woods, gorges, lakes and eccentric old buildings. It is also steeped in legend: male and female giants, caught up in a love triangle, are said to have formed the landscape from here down to Weston-super-Mare. The park covers 650 acres of grassland and woodland, owned and conserved by the City Council since 1926. 'Blaise offers a great package—dramatic scenery, a museum, a castle folly, two lakes and numerous paths to explore,' says Martin Harris, the estate manager. Facilities include a car park, café, toilets and a challenging play area.

On the highest point of the estate is an Iron Age enclosure, a Roman temple, a hill fort, and now Thomas Farr's Gothic style folly castle. The dedication and hard work of the Friends of Blaise is evident in their restoration of the castle. From the top floor, one of the Friends' founding members, Pat Clarke, proudly points out the Cotswolds, the Severn Bridges, the Welsh hills, Avon Gorge and the Clifton Suspension Bridge. 'It's said that Farr, who owned the Blaise Estate, built the castle to have the best possible view of his ships as they arrived in the Severn Estuary,' Pat explains.

The estate was designed in 1795 by landscape architect Humphry Repton, who used the dramatic scenery to best effect by creating view points and laying out paths. The drive from Coombe Dingle, for example, follows the Hazel Brook, enters the gorge, passes two lakes, a magnificent beech cathedral, and joins the drive from Henbury Lodge where it crosses the Brook and climbs up towards Mansion House. Other smaller paths lead to the castle, caves and the Giant's Footprint.

Magnificent oaks, cedars and maples are scattered across open grassland in front of Blaise Castle House, which now has a museum featuring a Victorian classroom and a Cabinet of Curiosities. An events programme for the estate ranges from music in the park to children's entertainers and craft workshops. Pat and Martin have heard many say that 'Blaise Castle Estate offers one of the best free days out in Bristol.'

Lawrence Weston Community Farm

Learning and inclusion down on the farm

In 1986 an enthusiastic group of Lawrence Weston residents joined together to transform a local council rubbish tip into a dynamic neighbourhood farm. Run as a community-managed project, the farm has been developed to improve the quality of life for local people and to combat social exclusion. Covering 7.5 acres, it now attracts 20,000 visitors a year to see the livestock and enjoy the outdoor space. The management committee makes a concerted effort to listen to local residents to ensure the farm is providing what the community wants. Working together, they offer a range of innovative educational and recreational activities that benefit the social, environmental and economic well-being of Lawrence Weston.

A visit to the farm gives you the opportunity to watch the large and small animals, and to see a bee apiary up close. There is also a secret garden with a polytunnel to explore, an outdoor soft play area for the summer months, a picnic area, orchard, duck pond, compost heaps, outdoor pig pen and chicken coop. August 2010 saw the opening of a new woodland walk alongside the three large paddocks. The farm offers volunteer placements and formal and informal training in subjects such as animal care, bee-keeping and gardening.

The committee are planning to produce more food on the farm, to teach people about food production, and to build better social and training facilities, including a café. Although the farm receives many visitors, it would love more engagement with the local community—people coming to buy produce and spread the word. There are opportunities at the farm to join the management committee and to develop business partnerships.

Southmead Development Trust

Business alongside well-being

The Greenway Centre is an old boy's school that was given to Southmead neighbourhood by Bristol City Council in 1990 to be run for the benefit of the local community. It is managed by the Southmead Development Trust (SDT), which comprises an elected board of local residents and a team of staff.

The Greenway Centre is now a well-developed resource for the community, with a fully equipped fitness suite, sports hall, dance studio, playing fields, café and a large hall with a stage. It has a small business centre that has permanent tenants as well as rooms for hire to the voluntary and private sector. Various groups use the centre's facilities on a regular basis including the Well-Being Choir, North Bristol Trampoline Club, dance groups, Westbury Art Club, a mother and toddler group, a holiday play scheme and the local Community Church. A Learndirect Training Suite offers courses to students wishing to improve their language, numeracy and IT skills.

One of the longest tenancies is held by Southmead Rugby Club, which boasts a thriving junior section and a recently refurbished clubhouse. Its neighbour on site is the Greenway Community Practice, a GP practice with a philosophy that embraces all aspects of well-being. Patients here may be referred to the fitness trainer in the gym or the Well-Being Choir along with NHS treatments.

The Greenway Centre is like an uncut gem that, after a bit of a polish, has the potential to shine. The new SDT board, elected in November 2009, are enthusiastic about making plans to set up a Saturday market and develop more arts activities. Even in these uncertain economic times there is determination to see the centre thrive and blossom into a resource that is responsive to the needs of Southmead residents and other communities beyond.

Sustainable Westbury-on-Trym

Using less, living more

One of Bristol's newest Transition groups, Sustainable Westbury-on-Trym (SusWot) made its mark with its EcoFiesta in September 2009. The high street in the village was closed to traffic and nearly a thousand locals enjoyed puppet theatre, bicycle-powered smoothie-making, stalls selling local produce, a lego street run on renewable energy, and a car having a 'duvet day'—a day off being driven. Residents were encouraged to sign eco-pledge leaves and view sketches of how the centre of the village could be made more pedestrian-friendly. 'We didn't know what reaction to expect from the fair,' says Andy O'Brien, who set up SusWot in 2008, 'but it went way beyond our expectations.' The feedback was so positive the EcoFiesta may become an annual event.

Andy was inspired to establish a local Transition group after years of working on campaigns for the World Development Movement and Jubilee 2000. Realising that climate change was the burning issue of our time, he wanted to make it part of mainstream concerns—not just that of minority environmental organisations. In line with other Transition groups, he and fellow SusWot members believe that resilience against global warming and peak oil is best achieved at the community level. So sustainability projects need to be more engaging and easy for everyone to join in.

The EcoFiesta certainly fits this bill, along with SusWot's other on-going projects, which include a monthly local produce market and the work of four subgroups: energy, transport, green spaces and waste reduction. The energy group is linking Westbury-on-Trym into Bristol Green Doors and to a project with the Energy Saving Trust that will help households reduce their energy costs by £300 a year. Also in the pipeline are community renewable energy projects, such as the pooled buying of solar panels.

Biodiversity is an interest of the green spaces group, with research being carried out into the healthiness of the River Trym, and a creepy-crawly species count in the open space around the medical centre. But SusWot's most ambitious project yet may be its plans to help re-introduce a people-centred vitality to the village high street—good for the community, good for businesses and good for local shoppers.

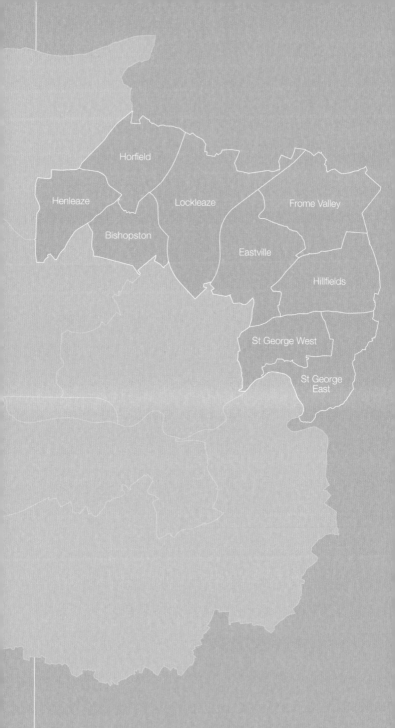

North East

This area of town stretches from the edge of South Gloucestershire in the north to the River Avon in the south-east. It encompasses several of Bristol's seven hills and sheltered among them are nine neighbourhoods, each with its own kind of good living.

On the western side, Henleaze has a secluded quarry lake open to avid swimmers and fishermen. In Horfield residents are partying together on the common and setting up food buying groups and community orchards. South from here, in Bishopston, runs the longest shopping street of independent retailers in the UK, the glorious Gloucester Road. Its residential area houses organisations such as Sustainable Bishopston, Grounds4Change and a group opposing the development of supermarkets. Up the hill, Lockleaze, once known as Bristol's 'forgotten community', is being revitalised by a new cycle path from the city centre, the Lockleaze Voice and by plans to open up Stoke Park and grow food on Sims Hill.

Across the M32 life changes as green, open spaces become more frequent in the residential areas of Frome Vale, Eastville and St George. These inspired the 'Parks and orchards' tour in this chapter, which features the Frome Valley Walkway that follows the river through watery rural landscapes. The Fishponds shopping area nearby has its own farmers market, a deli, café bars and a bustling atmosphere. Further over in Speedwell, Hillfields and St George the neighbourhoods are less cohesive but local organisations are being formed, such as the Friends of Troopers Hill and the Asylum Seekers Allotment project. These groups are taking the initiative to build closer communities and protect their neighbourhoods' natural resources.

Calm spaces and low-key shopping

Lined by independent shops, cafés and bars, Gloucester Road is one of the main arteries of this area and draws in residents from all the neighbourhoods around. This tour is good for browsing and for hanging out in cafés as you make your way gradually up the bustling street. One of the oldest stores on this stretch, and the start of this tour, is the Bishopston Trading Company where generations of ethical fashionistas have come to buy fairtrade and organic clothes. A little further on, there are numerous holistic therapies to choose from if you want a treat at the Healing Rooms. Otherwise, recharge your energy with some tasty vegetarian food at the World Peace Café before heading to Billie-Jean Clothes to try on some amazing old retro outfits.

You can jump on a bus at this point and hop off again at the Wellington pub (where there is a recently restored Victorian urinal—unmissable!). From here the tour crosses parkland to Horfield Common, where a friends group is working hard to create a space that attracts residents while also preserving wildlife. The tour ends about a half a mile further on at the Eden Grove Market and Café. Along with its community garden project, this centre has become a hub of neighbourhood employment and cohesion in Upper Horfield.

This tour will take around two hours if you catch the bus from Billie-Jean Clothes up to the Wellington pub. If you walk all the way it will take around three hours.

 **Where to start**

Bishopston Trading Company is a 10–15 minute bus ride or cycle from the city centre. Walking takes about 45 minutes up Gloucester Road. There is limited car parking in this shopping area.

For more travel information please refer to pp. 16–17.

Bishopston Trading Company

193 Gloucester Road, Bristol, BS7 8BG

Fairtrade company selling products made of certified organic cotton.

In 1978 a group of Bishopston residents twinned their neighbourhood with the South Indian village of K.V. Kuppam. The Bishopston Trading Company was set up to provide the people of K.V. Kuppam with skilled employment. The company now sells unique handmade products ranging from womenswear to children's bedding, toys and gifts.

From this store carry on up Gloucester Road to the traffic lights. Cross straight over and a little further along you will find the World Peace Café on the right, inside the Amitabha Buddhist Centre.

World Peace Café

Amitabha Buddhist Centre, Gloucester Road, Bishopston, Bristol, BS7 8NX

Serves light meals and snacks, teas, coffees and sumptuous hot chocolate.

Housed in the Amitabha Buddhist Centre, a space for meditation and learning, the café sells vegetarian meals along with cakes and drinks. Wherever possible the produce is organic and fairtrade. The café also provides free internet access, baby changing facilities and a peaceful garden.

Come out of the café and turn right to carry on up Gloucester Road. A few minutes further on cross over the road to find the Healing Rooms above the Bristol Buddhist Centre.

 ### The Healing Rooms

162 Gloucester Road, Bishopston, Bristol, BS7 8NT

A peaceful space with therapies for physical and emotional well-being.

The Healing Rooms has trained practitioners offering many different therapies. These include acupuncture, massage, hypnotherapy, Chinese herbal medicine and psychotherapy.

Again, head up Gloucester Road a short way to come to Billie-Jean Clothes on the same side of the road.

I ♥ Bristol because...

it's an easy-going multi-cultural city of free spirits and creativity.

 ### Billie-Jean Clothes

208 Gloucester Road, Bishopston, Bristol, BS7 8NU

Retro and party clothes and a wide selection of men's hats.

A fun and exciting vintage clothes store selling a range of retro and glamour garments and accessories to brighten up every wardrobe. You can also update your home with Billie-Jean's varied stock of throws, curtains and fabrics.

From here you can catch a bus heading up towards Horfield Common (ask to stop by the Wellington pub) or carry on walking or cycling up Gloucester Road for about a mile until you reach the Wellington pub on the left-hand side. Walk up Wellington Hill to arrive on Horfield Common at the junction with Kellaway Avenue.

Friends of Horfield Common

Off Kellaway Avenue

Volunteers who protect and develop this wonderful natural asset.

A group of local residents manages this historic common to ensure continued access and to improve its facilities. This includes coppicing trees, clearing ditches, installing new benches and bins, and organising a summer picnic. The common has a play area, wildlife pond and sports club.

After a relaxing break on a park bench or ambling around the Common head onto Kellaway Avenue—this time northwards toward the junction with Gloucester Road. Carry on up Gloucester Road for another half a mile, passing the Inn on the Green pub on your right and the new Orchard School on your left. Just after the school turn right into Eden Grove. Another couple of minutes along this road you will find the entrance to the Eden Market and Café through the Methodist Church Hall on your left.

 ## Eden Market and Café

UHCT Community Centre, Eden Grove, Horfield, Bristol, BS7 0PQ

Sells home-made bread, cake, jams, pickles and second-hand clothes.

See case study: 'Diversity and collaboration' on p. 187, which also relates to the Upper Horfield Community Trust listing.

From the café you may also be able to explore the community garden at the rear, which supplies some of its food. To go into town or on towards Filton and other areas in South Gloucestershire head to Filton Road or back to Gloucester Road to catch a bus or to cycle. Walking to town will take a couple of hours at a steady rate.

Snuff Mills

Parks and orchards

North-east Bristol has many green spaces where wildlife thrives, vegetables and fruit trees grow, and local residents make the most of the open air. This tour wends its way from one green space to the next, connecting up neighbourhoods as it goes. It starts on top of Troopers Hill, a nature reserve lying along the River Avon with stunning views across the east of the city. This is followed by the the neat avenues of trees and stately ornamental gates of St Georges Park. From here the tour takes you to the community orchards and allotments in Royate Hill and Fishponds—always keen for new members—before heading off to another splendid Victorian park in Eastville.

The route then returns to a nature reserve as it enters a part of the Frome Valley Walkway, which connects central Bristol to the source of the River Frome in the Cotswolds. Along here, at Snuff Mills, you can rest up at the tea room and try to glimpse a kingfisher from the river terrace. The tour makes a detour to Oldbury Court Estate from here—adding on a couple of miles—or you can continue on, under the M32, into Stoke Park, a long stretch of open land being made accessible by the Lockleaze group SPACE. If you still have energy at this point it's worth heading on a little further to see what's growing at the Sims Hill shared harvest scheme.

This is one of the longest tours in the guide, at five miles—or seven miles with the extra leg to Oldbury Court Estate. You may wish to cycle it but be aware that some sections require you to get off your bike and climb up and down steps and exit through gates. Cycling will take around one and a half hours, two hours including Oldbury Court Estate. Walking will take at least three hours.

⟶ Where to start

You can walk or cycle from Temple Meads station to Troopers Hill by following the National Cycle Network Route 3 along the River Avon for two miles, or you can take a bus from the city centre. There is limited car parking in this residential area.

For more travel information please refer to pp.16–17.

Orchard apples

I♥ Bristol because...
of Aardmann Animations, cheers Gromit!

1 Troopers Hill Nature Reserve

Friends of Troopers Hill, Troopers Hill Road, St George, Bristol, BS5 8BU

A haven for wildlife with a Green Flag award.

Only three miles from the city centre, Troopers Hill is a fantastic showcase for Bristol's biodiversity. Rare plants and invertebrates can be found here, along with many bird species and deer. The area was previously mined and quarried but is now protected by a dedicated local group.

Exit from Troopers Hill onto Malvern Road, taking the first right onto Diamond Road and then the first left onto Jubilee Road. At the junction with Beaufort Road cross over and then take the third left into Beaconsfield Road. At the end cross over Church Road to enter St Georges Park.

Friends of St Georges Park

Entrance: off Church Road.

Enthusiastic volunteer group maintaining and improving the park.

Large Victorian park with a lake, play area, tennis courts and skate park. The park has many mature trees and hundreds of younger ones added on tree planting days. The friends group, made up of local residents, works with the neighbourhood and the council to improve the park's facilities.

Leaving the park on Park Crescent go up Congleton Road to Whitehall Road. Take a left here until you reach Gordon Road. The most direct, if not picturesque, route to take is along Gordon Road until it changes into Rose Green Road. This follows the boundary of Greenbank Cemetery and goes under the Bristol and Bath Railway Path. Just after the bridge take a right by 45 Royate Hill into the Community Orchard (contact the orchard ahead of time if you wish to access it rather than just admiring the scene).

North East fact :

As many as 78% of respondents throughout Bristol have taken, or intend to take, action to tackle climate change.

3 Royate Hill Community Orchard

Royate Hill Allotment Site entrance: next to 45 Royate Hill, Bristol, BS5 6LP

Apple, pear and plum orchard in a permaculture allotment site.

This orchard has more than 100 fruit trees, including 40 varieties of apple. It has workdays on the first and third Saturday of each month and runs courses in pruning, grafting, apple pressing and cider making. Volunteers are also building a reciprocal frame roundhouse from local green timber.

Coming out of the orchard onto Royate Hill go right to reach Stonebridge Park. Carry on to the end of the road and turn left into Ridgeway Road. Crossing Fishponds Road carry straight on along Knowlsey Road to reach Fishponds Community Orchard (another place to call ahead of time to make the most of this tour).

I ♥ Bristol because...

people share gluts of fruit.

④ Fishponds Community Orchard

Thingwall Allotment Site, Thingwall Park, Fishponds, Bristol, BS16 3TE

Runs events and workshops for schools and the local community.

Bordering parkland that is home to more than 50 bird species, this lovely community orchard has a wide selection of fruit trees including many local apple varieties, such as the Berkeley Pippin. It is managed by volunteers and has regular workdays, wassailing and an annual Apple Day celebration.

Return to Fishponds Road and turn right to access Eastville Park a few minutes further on.

⑤ Eastville Park

Entrance: off Fishponds Road

Spacious, well-used park with a lake and a community garden.

Another fine Victorian city park, Eastville is popular as a football venue as well as boasting a lake, community garden, one-hundred-year-old bowling greens and an original Victorian drinking fountain. There is a wide variety of wildlife, including kingfishers, badgers and foxes.

Cross through the park in the direction of the M32. Just as you near the edge of the park by Stapleton Road take a path towards the right to join the Frome Valley Walkway. Follow this trail until it comes to Broomhill Road. Turning left follow this road until it crosses over into River View, from where you can access Snuff Mills.

6 Snuff Mills Action Group

Entrance: River View, Frenchay, Bristol, BS16

Conserves the beautiful wooded valley of Snuff Mills.

Lying on the river between Eastville Park and Oldbury Court Estate, Snuff Mills is named after the ruined mill found on the site. The action group works to improve Snuff Mills, Oldbury Court and Wickham Glen for people and wildlife, and campaigns against development in neighbouring fields and woodlands.

Following along the Frome Valley Walkway for 15 minutes or so you either have the option of carrying on to Oldbury Court Estate, which will add at least another hour to the tour, or turn back to Broomhill Road. At Broomhill Road turn right and continue to the top of the hill. Cross over to access a path that leads you under the M32 into Stoke Park.

How good does your street look? Many people would like some improvement, such as the 67% of respondents in St George.

7 Oldbury Court Estate

Oldbury Court Road, Fishponds, Bristol, BS16

Historic parkland, riverside paths, picnic areas and panoramic views.

Loved by families, walkers and wildlife enthusiasts, Oldbury Court is a large estate with fantastic views and great picnic spots. There are many woodland and riverside paths to explore, a children's play area and large open spaces for roaming.

If you've carried onto Oldbury Court on this tour you can follow your nose back through Snuff Mills and follow the directions from there onto Stoke Park. Alternatively, you may like to carry on to Frenchay Road and follow Pearces Hill and Begbrook Park onto Frenchay Park Road, turning left to follow the road until the path opposite the end of Broomhill Road. This path will take you under the M32.

8 Stoke Park Adult Community Entertainment Nature Reserve

Entrance: off Romney Avenue

Wild food walks, green woodwork courses, bush craft skills and more.

See case study: 'Putting a park on the map' on p. 186.

Emerging from underneath the M32 you come out into a beautiful open space with the big yellow Dower House perched on the hill in front of you. Follow the path up parallel to the house and come out onto Jellicoe Avenue. Pass through the housing estate to Coldharbour Lane. To visit the next location you will need to arrange a meeting with the community group that have set up Sims Hill Shared Harvest. They will normally meet people nearby on Stoke Lane to lead them into the site.

9 Sims Hill Shared Harvest

Off Sims Hill, Frenchay, Bristol, BS16 1QG

Produces good quality fruit and vegetables on historic agricultural land.

A new Community Supported Agriculture initiative, Sims Hill Shared Harvest will provide members with fruit and vegetables grown in the Bristol area using natural farming methods. The project aims to re-establish local food supply chains and create an enriching partnership between people and the land.

From the Sims Hill site go back towards Stoke Park to connect to a cycle path that leads into the centre of town, or catch a bus from Coldharbour Lane.

Directory

 ## Asylum Seekers Allotment Project

Between 44 and 46 Speedwell Road, Speedwell, Bristol, BS5
urbanvegtim@yahoo.co.uk

Celebrates different cultures through growing food.

See case study: 'Fertile sanctuaries' on p. 183.

 ## Avon Organic Group

Meetings held at: The Friends Meeting House, 300 Gloucester Road,
Bristol, BS7
membership@avonorganicgroup.org.uk
www.avonorganicgroup.org.uk

Long-standing organic gardening group that runs the Horfield
Community Orchard.

 ## The Bay Tree

176 Henleaze Road, Henleaze, Bristol, BS9 4NE
0117 962 1115

Shop and restaurant specialising in healthy, natural, organic foods.

 ## Begbrook Green Park

Frenchay Park Road, Frenchay, Bristol, BS16
0117 922 3719

Community park with fruit trees managed by a local group.

Billie-Jean Clothes

208 Gloucester Road, Bishopston, Bristol, BS7 8NU
0117 944 5353
billie@billiejeanclothes.com
www.billiejeanclothes.com

Retro and party clothes and a wide selection of men's hats.

Bishopston Opposing Glut of Supermarkets (BOGOFS)

PO Box 241, 82 Colston Street, Bristol, BS1 5BB
www.bogofs.org

Group of local residents opposing supermarket development.

Bishopston Society

www.bishopstonsociety.org.uk

Maintains and improves the character, amenities and architecture of the area.

Bishopston Trading Company

193 Gloucester Road, Bristol, BS7 8BG
0117 924 5598
mail@bishopstontrading.co.uk
www.bishopstontrading.co.uk

Fairtrade company selling products made of certified organic cotton.

Bristol Community Housing Foundation

400 Filton Avenue, Bristol, BS7 0LJ
0117 947 0501
info@bchf.co.uk
www.bchf.co.uk

Social housing provider giving tenants a stronger voice.

BCHF is a not-for-profit housing association building affordable, community-led homes across Bristol. They aim to create attractive neighbourhoods where people choose to live, with well-designed houses and high eco-standards.

Bristol Nappies

07834 319993
vicky@bristolnappies.co.uk
http://bristolnappies.co.uk

Business offering everything to do with reusable nappies.

A Bristol-based company set up by one mum with the intention of promoting the economic and environmental benefits of cloth nappies. The online store sells cloth nappies and has a range of FAQs for anxious parents confused by all the nappy options.

Bristol Natural Health Service

407 Gloucester Road, Bristol, BS7 8TS
0117 944 4448
www.bristol-natural-health-service.co.uk

Offers alternative and complementary therapies and medicines.

Castellano's

802 Fishponds Road, Fishponds, Bristol, BS16 3TE
0117 965 2792
deli@castellanos.co.uk
www.castellanos.co.uk

Family-run deli with handmade and locally sourced produce.

Earth Abbey Walled Garden

60 Barton Hill Road, Barton Hill, Bristol, BS5 9TJ
chris.sunderland@agoraspace.org

Protected permaculture growing space for plants and people.

Ebenezer Church

286 Filton Avenue, Horfield, Bristol, BS7 0BA
0117 979 1399
www.ebe.org.uk

Involved with many community clubs and activities for local residents.

 ## Eden Market and Café

UHCT Community Centre, Eden Grove, Horfield, Bristol, BS7 0PQ
0117 969 0011
maria@uhct.co.uk
http://uhct.co.uk

Sells home-made bread, cake, jams, pickles and second-hand clothes.

See case study: 'Diversity and collaboration' on p. 187.

I ♥ Bristol because...

Open spaces around the city can be seen from everywhere.

 ## Essential Trading Cooperative

Unit 3 Lodge Causeway Trading Estate, Fishponds, Bristol, BS16 3JB
0117 958 3550
contact-us@essential-trading.coop
www.essential-trading.coop

Manufactures and distributes organic wholefoods and ecological household products.

See case study: 'Democratic, organic and fair' on p. 184.

Fishponds Community Orchard

Thingwall Allotment Site, Thingwall Park, Fishponds, Bristol, BS16 3TE
0117 965 8429
iblessitt@hotmail.com

Runs events and workshops for schools and the local community.

 ## Fishponds Farmers Market

Vassells Park, off Straits Parade, Fishponds, Bristol, BS16 2LA
01453 321010

Monthly market for local producers in Vassells Park.

Only 23% of respondents across Bristol think they can influence decisions in their neighbourhood.

 ## Friends of Horfield Common

Entrance: off Kellaway Avenue
cjt10rr@hotmail.com
www.friendsofhorfieldcommon.com

Volunteers who protect and develop this wonderful natural asset.

 ## Friends of St Georges Park

Entrance: off Church Road
0117 939 4816
ramelhammer@hotmail.com
http://stgeorgepark.blogspot.com

Enthusiastic volunteer group maintaining and improving the park.

 ## GRAB Gloucester Road Alternative Bag Campaign

Gloucester Road, Bristol, BS7
07947 577503
grab.campaign@gmail.com
www.lovegloucesterroad.org.uk

Local residents and traders campaigning to make Gloucester Road plastic-bag free.

 Grounds4Change

Dovercourt Depot, Dovercourt Road, Bristol, BS7 9SH
0117 969 3815
www.grounds4change.co.uk

Improves and restores gardens, open spaces and parks.

An organisation that works to improve Bristol's environment by helping communities improve their open spaces. It tailors its methods to different groups and offers environmental youth work projects, community clean-ups, landscape gardening and support for building 'living classrooms' in schools.

 The Healing Rooms

162 Gloucester Road, Bishopston, Bristol, BS7 8NT
www.healingroomsbristol.co.uk

A peaceful space with therapies for physical and emotional well-being.

 Henleaze Lake

Lake Road, Henleaze, Bristol, BS10 5HY
0117 962 0696
www.henleazeswimmingclub.org

Secluded quarry lake for swimming, diving and angling (members only).

 Henleaze Society

derek.wilding@btinternet.com
www.henleazesociety.co.uk

Founded in 1973, the society ensures Henleaze remains a good place to live and work.

 Horfield Organic Community Orchard

25 Wolseley Road, Horfield, Bristol, BS7 8EL
0117 373 1587
info.orchard@avonorganicgroup.org.uk
www.avonorganicgroup.org.uk/orchard

Grows a wide range of fruit, with members sharing the harvest.

See case study: 'Fresh urban fruit' on p. 185.

 ## Indras-Net

31 Birchall Road, Bishopston, Bristol, BS6 7TW
0117 924 6344
cathy@indras-net.co.uk

Network of facilitators and trainers using consensus building for
sustainable development.

 ## Kondi Café

103–105 Henleaze Road, Henleaze, Bristol, BS9 4JP
0117 962 8230

Popular family-run café with home-made food.

 ## Lockleaze and Horfield Strollers

0117 352 1283
nicola.ferris@bristol.gov.uk
www.bristol.gov.uk/healthwalks

Walks for all ages and abilities in Lockleaze and other areas of Bristol.

 ## Lockleaze Neighbourhood Trust

The Cameron Centre, Cameron Walk, Lockleaze, Bristol, BS7 9XB
0117 914 1129
info@lockleazent.co.uk
www.lockleazeneighbourhoodtrust.co.uk

Works with the local community to address its needs.

This small charity, backed by members of the Lockleaze community,
maximises investment in the area and enables local people to develop
skills and grow in self-confidence. The trust manages the Cameron Centre
and the Blake Centre, where it runs several activities as well as a
community kitchen.

 ## Lockleaze Voice

swadmin@planningaid.rtpi.org.uk
http://lockleazevoice.org.uk

Community group ensuring that residents' views about local development
are heard.

I ♥ Bristol because...

You don't need much money to enjoy this city.

 ## Lockleaze Youth and Play Space

Romney Avenue, Lockleaze, Bristol, BS7 9SU
0117 352 1394
charlene.richardson@bristol.gov.uk
www.goplacesdothings.org.uk

Activities for teenagers and an adventure playground for younger children.

 ## Logos House Allotment

Logos House, Wade Street, Bristol, BS2 9EL
chris.sunderland@agoraspace.org

Healthly-living allotment for the homeless hostel.

 ## North Bristol Community Project – One in Eight

160 Gloucester Road, Bishopston, Bristol, BS7 8NT
0117 924 6228
northbristolcommunityproject@yahoo.co.uk
www.oneineight.co.uk

Adult education project offering classes in art, languages and IT.

 ## Oldbury Court Estate

Oldbury Court Road, Fishponds, Bristol, BS16
0117 922 3719
bristolparks@bristol.gov.uk

Historic parkland, riverside paths, picnic areas and panoramic views.

On Your Bike

UHCT Community Centre, Eden Grove, Horfield, Bristol, BS7 0PQ
0117 969 0011
oyb@mail.com
www.oyb.moonfruit.com

Training programme to make cycling more accessible in the area.

 ## Osna Therapy Centre

234 Gloucester Road, Bishopston, Bristol, BS7 8NZ
bridget@osna.co.uk
www.osna.co.uk

Range of treatments centering around aromatherapy, reflexology and massage.

 ## Royate Hill Community Orchard

Royate Hill Allotment Site entrance: next to 45 Royate Hill, Bristol, BS5 6LP
07768 915423
mikefeingold@blueyonder.co.uk

Apple, pear and plum orchard in a permaculture allotment site.

 ## Royate Hill Nature Reserve

Royate Hill Nature Reserve entrance: on Edward Street, Eastville, Bristol, BS5 6LW
0117 917 7270
mail@avonwildlifetrust.org.uk
www.avonwildlifetrust.org.uk

Old orchard, meadow, stream and young woodland.

Sims Hill Shared Harvest

Off Sims Hill, Frenchay, Bristol, BS16 1QG
simshillsharedharvest@googlemail.com
http://simshillsharedharvest.wordpress.com

Producing good-quality fruit and vegetables on historic agricultural land.

Snuff Mills Action Group

Entrance: River View, Frenchay, Bristol, BS16
snuffmills@hotmail.co.uk

Conserves the beautiful wooded valley of Snuff Mills.

 ## St George Community Centre

**St George Community Centre, Church Road, St George,
Bristol, BS5 8AA**
07757 319582
www.stgeorgecc.co.uk

Actively involved in many local projects with rooms available for hire.

 ## Stoke Park Adult Community Entertainment

Entrance: off Romney Avenue
07789 943114
alex.wood@nhs.net

Wild food walks, green woodwork courses, bush craft skills and more.

See case study: 'Putting a park on the map' on p. 186.

 ## Sustainable Bishopston

info@sustainablebishopston.org.uk
www.sustainablebishopston.org.uk

Residents group running local projects to combat climate change.

 ## Troopers Hill Nature Reserve

**Friends of Troopers Hill, Troopers Hill Road, St George,
Bristol, BS5 8BU**
0117 922 3719
friends@troopers-hill.org.uk
www.troopers-hill.org.uk

A haven for wildlife with a Green Flag award.

Upper Horfield Community Gardening Club

UHCT Community Centre, Eden Grove, Horfield, Bristol, BS7 0PQ

0117 969 0011

scott@bchf.co.uk

http://uhcgc.wordpress.com

Cultivates fruit and vegetables in the grounds of Eden Grove church.

Upper Horfield Community Trust

UHCT Community Centre, Eden Grove, Horfield, Bristol, BS7 0PQ

0117 969 0011

maria@uhct.co.uk

www.uhct.co.uk

Charity working to bring together the diverse Horfield community.

See case study: 'Diversity and collaboration' on p. 187.

Wizard Compton

C/o Melody House 253, Filton Avenue, Bristol, BS7 0QF

0117 949 7742

www.wizardcompton.org.uk

Wizard playing an original Compton Theatre organ at the Methodist Church Hall.

World Development Movement Bristol

Horfield Quaker Meeting House, 300 Gloucester Road, Bristol, BS7 8PD

0117 924 1304

phillada@blueyonder.co.uk

www.wdm.me.uk/bristol

Local branch of national organisation tackling the underlying causes of poverty.

World Peace Café

Amitabha Buddhist Centre, Gloucester Road, Bishopston, Bristol, BS7 8NX

0117 974 5160

info@meditationinbristol.org

www.meditationinbristol.org/WorldPeaceCafe

Serves light meals and snacks, teas, coffees and sumptuous hot chocolate.

Asylum Seekers Allotment Project

Fertile sanctuaries

On four allotment plots just off Speedwell Road 50 different kinds of vegetables are grown by a group of volunteer asylum seekers. Established in April 2009, the Asylum Seekers Allotment Project (ASAP) is a young initiative with huge potential, not only for refugees but for society more widely. Within the borders of this fertile garden is a space for alienated, disenfranchised individuals to connect with the land and with each other while cultivating fresh, nutritious produce to share.

Tim Lawrence, who had the idea for the project and is its coordinator and lead grower, believes that working the soil can give people a sense of dignity and connectedness that supports them in other aspects of their lives. For asylum seekers who are struggling with legal battles or dealing with past traumas gardening in the allotment can be very therapeutic. 'It's a social space,' says Tim, 'but they don't have to talk.' He mentions one Kurdish volunteer from Iran who joined ASAP highly stressed and anxious but now, much calmer, has taken the lead in cooking communal meals from the allotment produce. For a Somalian volunteer the project has also provided purpose and now with full legal status, he is doing a community work apprenticeship to become qualified to work with refugees himself.

ASAP has only taken off, however, due to the effective partnerships it has developed with Bristol Refugee Rights and the Bristol Hospitality Network. These organisations have provided the links to connect disparate asylum seekers to the allotment. Some of the volunteers live with friends, others with host families or in hostels where they share their weekly bag of fresh vegetables. The Earth Abbey Walled Garden project in Barton Hill has also proved an invaluable partner as it has polytunnels in which peppers, aubergines, okra and other vegetables—often familiar to the volunteers from their home countries—can be cultivated.

Out of a derelict, bramble-covered site Tim and his first team of volunteers have established a productive, nurturing enterprise that is now ready to absorb a wider group. Funds have been limited, but dedication and imagination plentiful, and the project will be a sanctuary of calm for many more asylum seekers to come.

Essential Trading Cooperative

Democratic, organic and fair

Essential was born when two long-standing cooperatives, Harvest Natural Foods based in Bath and Nova wholefoods of Bristol, merged in 1991. It is the largest worker cooperative in Bristol and is dedicated to distributing organic, fairtrade, sustainable and ethical wholefoods. Essential currently has 80 members and 20 probationers (who will become members after working there for eight months). With each member having an equal share of the company there is no hierarchy among employees. Eli, who has been a member for five years, loves the work environment, which she says is innovative and always interesting: 'Every single day people ask for new things. There's a constant influx of ideas and enterprises.'

The growing interest in organic and fairtrade products has seen Essential double in size since 2000. Rising to the demand for more sustainably sourced products, it sells many teas that are farmed on reclaimed desert and that boast a biodynamic label. Rose Elliot, the renowned vegetarian and astrologer, has endorsed Essential's products at the Natural Product show and written recipes for the cooperative.

Essential was among the pioneers of the fairtrade campaign and the anti-GM movement. It has its fingers in local pies as well, supporting ventures such as Ecomotive, Bristol's sustainable housing cooperative. Although it is mainly a wholesaler, Essential has two retail shops in the West Country (named Harvest after the original 1970s cooperative), one on Gloucester Road and one in Bath. Alongside Essential products both shops stock a range of local deli produce and fruit and veg.

The cooperative also sells to buying groups, which can be just a few neighbours in a street or several local organisations clubbing together to buy products in bulk. Essential is able to offer advice on setting up such a group, which can save a family 25 per cent on their weekly food bill.

Horfield Organic Community Orchard

Fresh urban fruit

This community orchard was set up in 1998 in some neglected allotment plots on the margins of the Horfield and District Allotment Association site. Initially ten fruit trees were recovered from the brambles but thanks to a committed group of local residents the orchard is now home to more than a hundred trees including apple, pear, plum, cherry, medlar, nut, apricot, peach, nectarine and fig, not to mention red, black and white currant bushes, grape vines, blueberries and gooseberries. All the working members are volunteers who share responsibility for all aspects of the orchard management, and in return enjoy fresh, naturally grown fruit much of the year. If you would like to become involved in the orchard, membership is open to members of the Avon Organic Group or the Horfield and District Allotment Association. Alternatively, you can become a supporter by joining as a friend.

Each year the orchard is open to the public to celebrate Apple Day, which takes place on the Saturday before 21 October, and again in May to enjoy the blossom. These are popular events where people can learn about the skills needed to create and manage an orchard. Working members are happy to share their horticultural and community development knowledge at other times too. There are regular training workshops, as well as international and national hosted visits. This community orchard is part of a wider local food network and many of its members are involved with other food projects. They share the vision of Bristol as an edible urban garden helping the city to prosper in a greener, cleaner and more community-rooted way.

SPACE

Putting a park on the map

SPACE (Stoke Park Adult Community Entertainment) has been active in the Lockleaze area since April 2010. Led by Steve England, an RHS horticulturist, and Alex Wood from NHS community development the aim of the group is to open up the splendour of Stoke Park to the local population. SPACE organises a wide range of fun and educational activities in the park, but also encourages people to make the most of the green space for themselves.

Stoke Park is a mysterious place that does not feature on many maps. Until recently the land was owned by a private group of property developers; now it is in the process of being handed over to the City Council. Steve England, who has lived in the economically deprived Lockleaze all his life, believes that bringing the local community into the park will help people gain greater enjoyment from their surroundings and understand the environment better. To encourage this, SPACE runs regular activities such as wild walks, green woodwork workshops and history walks.

Interest in the group has been high, from people of all ages and backgrounds. 'People couldn't understand that there is this amazing park and no one knew about it,' says Steve. 'Even those who did weren't sure if they were allowed in.' SPACE has become a template for work with the local youth services, which now offer a gardening club where young people can tend their own allotments. Steve stresses that encouraging children to use open spaces such as Stoke Park, and teaching them skills such as making their own natural fertilisers, can really inspire them and plant a seed of interest in the environment for their future.

SPACE plans to expand its work with the youth services by carrying on workshops through the summer. The group is also starting to work with a local filmmaker to make a documentary about Stoke Park. The idea of SPACE was originally aimed at the Lockleaze community but now it has taken off they are keen to expand it, and enable far more people to enjoy and celebrate this lovely open parkland.

Upper Horfield Community Trust

Diversity and collaboration

This charitable trust collaborates with a number of local organisations to bring together the diverse community of Upper Horfield. This part of town has seen large-scale change over the past ten years, with the population almost doubling in size. Once a predominantly white area it is now increasingly multicultural. The Upper Horfield Community Trust (UHCT) works with the Bristol Community Housing Foundation and Orchard School Bristol, among others, to improve facilities and ensure that services are available to this growing number of diverse residents.

Situated in the heart of Upper Horfield, UHCT runs a community centre that offers after-school activities, computer classes, a cycling accessibility project, a community festival and community trading post. It has rooms for hire both in its own building and in partnership with Eden Grove Methodist Church, who own the land accommodating the centre. The Eden Café and Market are based at the centre too, offering well-priced meals alongside home-made produce and good-quality second-hand clothes. This provides an ideal space for interaction between different members of the community, as well as employing a number of locals.

To add to this diverse mix of activities, one of the last remaining wizard organs in the UK is located at the centre, and its player and carer, Byron Compton, often plays recitals to silent movies. Trying to make ends meet has led to an entrepreneurial spirit among UHCT staff and trustees. One of the centre's projects, the community trading post, sells items for local people on ebay in return for 20 per cent of the sale.

Another project making a mark here is the community garden in the grounds of the church. Now two years old, the gardening club grows fruit, vegetables and herbs, with members paying just £5 a year for an 8 by 4 foot bed. Gardeners cultivate half their plot for themselves and half for the café and market shop, which sell the produce to raise funds for other local services. Anyone local with gardening skills is warmly invited to come along and share them, or for those who have never grown food before, the community garden is a great place to start.

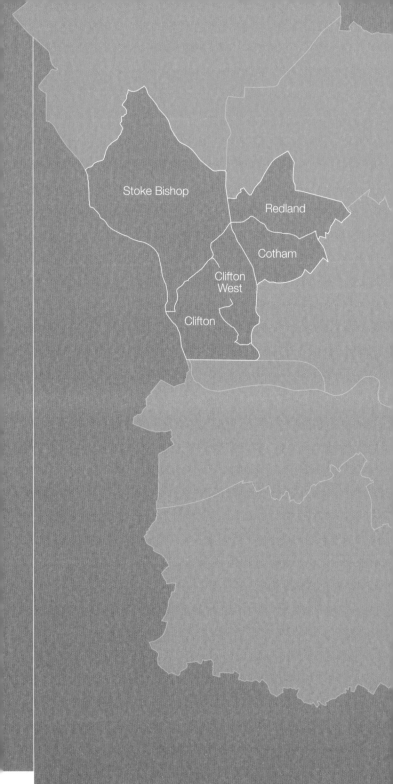

Stoke Bishop

Redland

Cotham

Clifton
West

Clifton

North Central

The phrase 'ship shape and Bristol fashion' brings maritime links to mind, but it also reflects the part of town that is, to many people, most recognisably Bristolian—Clifton. With its magnificent Suspension Bridge hanging across the Avon Gorge, the vast expanse of the Downs and the grandeur of Royal Crescent this area is synonymous with high-end good living.

More than other areas of town North Central has the wealth to buy into organic, renewable and low-impact lifestyles—and there are signs of this emerging in some shops and cafés. Down the hill from Clifton, Hotwells and Cliftonwood are making headway with their Transition group and Community Association. Residents here come out in force if developers show too much attention to their much-loved open spaces.

To the north-east, Cotham and Redland are closely connected to Gloucester Road and the many sustainability initiatives and social enterprises around here. Sustainable Redland is one of the key neighbourhood projects in this area, along with the Metford Road Community Orchard. In these leafy streets families go about their everyday business, quietly recycling their waste and getting on their bikes to work. North of Clifton, Stoke Bishop, which hugs the Avon Gorge and the Downs, enjoys the highest quality of life in the city, in terms of health, wealth and happiness. This area is connected to the water at Sea Mills and has many green open spaces that are well cared for by local residents.

Downs and hills

This tour snakes up, down and around several of Bristol's hills and green open spaces. The first stretch takes you from one of Cotham's bustling shopping streets, where chef Keith Floyd once had a restaurant, and on to the small but perfectly formed Cotham Gardens. From here you pass through the beautiful sloping park of St Andrews before heading over to the large and glorious Downs. In between these green expanses are some characterful buildings worth noting, such as the tiny art deco Orpheus Cinema on Northumbria Drive. These add to the history and culture of the different neighbourhoods. As you pass through each one—Cotham, Redland, Westbury Park, Sneed Park—you will notice how distinctive they all are, and how each feels like its own village.

This is a hilly tour so walking might be the easiest way to go round, though if you are a Bristolian try cycling it to really feel the ups and downs that shape this city. Walking the route will take a good few hours so make sure you stop at a few places for refreshments along the way—there are many independent cafés to choose from with good coffee and fresh, seasonal food. Cycling the tour will take an hour or so, or longer if you want to pause along the way to get a proper flavour of the place.

 Where to start

Bristol Kitestore is a ten minute bus or bike ride from the city centre, or a 40-minute walk up Park Street and Whiteladies Road, then turning off into Cotham Hill. There is limited car parking in this shopping and residential area.

For more travel information please refer to pp. 16–17.

1 Bristol Kitestore

39a Cotham Hill, Cotham, Bristol, BS6 6JY

Sells a wide array of kite-surfing, power and stunt kites.

A shop to bring out the inner child in everyone, this store offers a staggering variety of kites, including toy and stunt kites along with

The café in St Andrews Park

landboards, buggies and kite-surfing apparatus. It also has a good selection of circus equipment.

From Cotham Hill take a turning into Abbotsford Road, then a right into Hampton Road. Turn left into Ravenswood Road to come out into Redland Grove opposite Cotham Gardens.

 Cotham Gardens

Off Redland Grove, Redland, Bristol, BS6

Lovely, intimate park in the heart of a leafy residential neighbourhood.

A small Victorian park, this is one of the first public gardens created in Bristol. Packed with flowers and trees it is a good place for walks and picnics near the city centre, and it has a play area for children.

From Redland Grove go over the bridge and take a right behind Redland station. Follow Zetland Road all the way to the junction with Gloucester Road, opposite the Prince of Wales pub. Carry on up Gloucester Road for five minutes and you will come to Scoopaway on the right.

 Scoopaway

113 Gloucester Road, Bristol, BS7 8AT

Sells organic, vegetarian and wholefood produce by the scoopful.

Good value store stocking a wide range of dried foodstuffs. Like a healthy pick 'n' mix shop, you scoop what you need from the bins and pay by weight, avoiding over-packaging. It also sells environmentally sound beauty and hygiene products.

St Andrews Park can be reached either by walking through the Cooperative supermarket and then heading up Grenville Road, or by walking up Gloucester Road for one block, turning right into Somerville Road and then right into Effingham Road, where the park will be just ahead of you.

 Friends of St Andrews Park

St Andrews Park, Effingham Road, St Andrews, Bristol, BS6 5BA

Maintain the park as a cherished asset for the local community.

A voluntary group of dedicated individuals, the Friends maintain this beautiful Victorian park in the heart of St Andrews. There is a play area, children's paddling pool, bowling green and many mature trees dotted across the slopes. Regular events, such as bird walks, are held in and around the park.

Go back the way you came to Scoopaway, head down Gloucester Road and cross over to Claremont Road. Follow this street as it turns into Claremont Avenue. At the end turn left onto Clare Avenue and then right onto busy Cranbrook Road. Walk along for a few minutes then cross over and take a left into Harcourt Road, followed by another left into Metford Road. Walk to the turning with Cossins Road to find the entrance to the Metford Road Community Orchard (open by appointment only).

 Metford Road Community Orchard

Metford Road, Redland, Bristol, BS6 7LA

Thriving orchard run by volunteers from around Redland.

Created out of five abandoned allotments, the orchard is a wild place full of all kinds of fruit trees and bushes, and home to masses of butterflies, other insects and frogs. There are regular work days for members, pruning and grafting workshops, open-day picnics, apple days and other events.

From the orchard come out onto Cossins Road, go straight up Greendale Road to Coldharbour Road. Cross over and take the first left into St Alban's Road. At the end go left onto Linden Road and past Waitrose to find the Orpheus Cinema just beyond.

Orpheus Cinema

Northumbria Drive, Henleaze, Bristol, BS9 4HN

1930s cinema showing a film programme for all ages.

A much-loved old neighbourhood cinema screening films for all the family. With its art deco staircase, red velvet seats, cheap tickets and friendly atmosphere, the Orpheus is well worth a trip. Check out its show times to catch a matinée while you're on this tour.

From Northumbria Drive take a right after Waitrose and go along North View to Westbury Road. At the roundabout go straight ahead to enter the Downs.

7 The Downs

Off Stoke Road, Clifton, Bristol, BS9

Very popular open parkland between Clifton and Westbury Park.

The Downs are made up of Clifton Down and Durdham Down. A huge open space of around 400 acres, with fantastic views of Leigh Woods and the Avon Gorge, they are hugely are popular for sport, wildlife spotting and picnics.

Once in the Downs you have lots of space to skip around, play frisbee or have a rounders match. Crossing this area is a lovely walk in itself. Head south-west towards the Avon Gorge either by following your nose or by heading for Ladies Mile, reached via Saville Road and Stoke Road. Almost at the bottom of Ladies Mile you come to Circular Road on the right, which swoops around the edge of the Downs just above the gorge.

8 Avon Gorge and Downs Wildlife Project

Education Department, Bristol Zoo Gardens, Clifton Down, Bristol, BS8 3HA

Events and activities protecting wildlife in this area.

This project was set up in 1999 to protect the unique biodiversity of the Downs and Gorge, and to raise awareness of this internationally important wildlife site. The project carries out wildlife surveys and monitoring, habitat management and education.

From Circular Road go onto Ivywell Road, following it as it changes into Hazelwood Road. At Church Road turn left and then first right into Old Sneed Park. Take a left onto Glenavon Park and then follow the road round until you find the entrance to Old Sneed Park itself.

9 Friends of Old Sneed Park Nature Reserve

Entrance: south-east corner of Glenavon Park, Stoke Bishop, Bristol, BS9 1RN

Voluntary group that runs this beautiful council-owned nature reserve.

Sneed (confusingly also spelt Sneyd) Park was previously home to a deer park and is a valuable area for wildlife, including owls, badgers, kingfishers and butterflies. The Friends of Old Sneed Park Nature Reserve was established in 1995 and promotes wildlife education and conservation.

From Old Sneed Park the nearest bus stop is on Stoke Hill a few minutes walk away. If you are on a bike head towards the Downs again for routes across the city.

Clifton culture

Pick a sunny afternoon for this tour so you can amble slowly along Clifton's wide Georgian streets and enjoy the magnificent views. But don't worry if it starts to rain—there are plenty of places to stop for a cuppa, browse books or linger over vintage clothing. Clifton is the destination for many a tourist and local alike. Brunel's iconic Suspension Bridge is, of course, a major attraction, but this tour pairs such renowned tourist sites with more locally known gems. The second-hand clothes store Recession and the Boston Tea Party café, situated either side of Brandon Hill, are fine examples of Bristol's independent and family-run enterprises. Meanwhile, the Clifton Lido and Bristol Zoo Gardens are two delightful locations that have made big, and inspired, changes in recent years.

There is a strong sense of history on this tour. The pond gardens of Brandon Hill, the grandeur of the Wills Memorial Building (opposite the Oxfam bookshop) and the hill-top Observatory all point to people and times past that continue to shape the culture and identity of the city. Enjoy both the historical spots and the lively new enterprises as you wander through this beautiful part of town.

Taking time to walk this tour is well worth it, especially as parts of it have steps and places where you cannot ride your bike. It should take around three hours to walk if you stop in a few places, or an hour and a half if you steam through all the sights.

 Where to start

The bottom of Jacobs Wells Road is a five-minute walk from the city centre, even quicker by bike. By bus, get off at the bottom of Park Street, walk across College Green, past the Cathedral and on to the end of St Georges Road. At the end take a right to find Recession just after the roundabout.

For more travel information please refer to pp. 16–17.

Clifton Lido

① Recession

8 Jacobs Wells Road, Bristol, BS8 1EA

Second-hand clothes shop with some vintage gems.

See case study: 'A new lease of life' on p. 212.

Head up Jacobs Wells Road and take a right up some steps before the Avon Wildlife Trust Building. Follow a path around Brandon Hill and make your way up to Cabot Tower for stunning views of the city.

I ♥ Bristol because...
Bristol has two lungs – the Downs and the Docks.

② Friends of Brandon Hill

Off Jacobs Wells Road

Community group supporting the management of this ancient park.

Brandon Hill may be the oldest municipal park in the country, having been owned and run by various Bristol councils since 1174. Straddling a hillside in the city centre, it has ponds, a wildflower meadow, many mature trees and an old lookout tower. Popular for picnics, walking and watching the sunset, the park is well-maintained by the Friends group.

From Cabot Tower take the path onto Charlotte Street and at the end turn left into Park Street to find Boston Tea Party just up the hill.

I ♥ Bristol because...
just saying Bristol makes you happy!

③ Boston Tea Party

75 Park Street, Bristol, BS1 5PF

Popular West Country café using sustainably sourced produce.

A family-run enterprise, this café has delicious fresh food made largely from local, organic and fairtrade produce. It has a convivial upstairs seating area with sofas and large windows, and a quiet garden patio behind. Besides the one in Park Street there are Boston Tea Party cafés in Clifton Village and on Whiteladies Road.

Staying on this side of the road, carry on up Park Street to the traffic lights where you will find the Oxfam Books and Music shop.

④ Oxfam Books and Music

Queens Road, Bristol, BS8 1QE

Wide range of books and music, and ethically sourced food and gifts.

An exciting find for book lovers, this shop has an astonishing variety of literature, including classics, comics and non-fiction. The music section is complete with vinyl, CDs and sheet music. Recently, several valuable books were donated, including Theodore Duret's *Manet and the French Impressionists* containing original etchings by Manet and possibly worth over £1,000.

From Park Street go up Queen's Road until you come to Richmond Hill on your left. Follow this road until you reach the roundabout. Turn right here into St Paul's Road, then take a left onto Oakfield Grove to come out by the Lido on Oakfield Place.

5 Clifton Lido

Metford Road, Redland, Bristol, BS6 7LA

Restored Victorian lido with restaurant, spa, swimming pool and poolside bar.

Hidden in the Clifton back streets, this recently refurbished lido dates back to 1849. The solar-heated outdoor pool is perfectly complemented by a chic bar and restaurant serving sumptuous seasonal dishes. The venue also has a spa offering holistic treatments and a sauna, steam room, sundeck and spa pool.

From Oakfield Place go back on yourself to St Paul's Road and the roundabout. Go up Queen's Road and past the Bristol University Student's Union to arrive at the corner of Victoria Square. Enter the square on the paved path that crosses the gardens diagonally.

Did you know?

Families in Redland, Bishopston and Cotham are very happy with the children's playgrounds in their area—79% of respondents would like to say thank you!

6 Victoria Square and Gardens

Victoria Square, Clifton, Bristol, BS8 4ES

Tree-filled Georgian square and gardens with an archway into Clifton Arcade.

Rows of grand Georgian houses, designed to look like palaces, enclose this much-admired Clifton square. In the centre is a beautiful public garden with huge old trees. The square leads into Clifton Village and the Clifton Arcade, a recently restored Victorian arcade housing intriguing shops and a great bistro.

Go through the gardens and enter Clifton Village via the archway. The most scenic route from here is to go across Clifton Down Road and down Princess Victoria Street. Follow the street to the very end and take a right onto Sion Hill. The Suspension Bridge will appear up ahead of you.

7 Clifton Suspension Bridge Trust

Bridge Road, Leigh Woods, Bristol, BS8 3PA

Information centre and dramatic views of the Avon Gorge.

A renowned symbol of Bristol, the Suspension Bridge was designed by the great Isambard Kingdom Brunel in 1831, who died before it was completed in 1864. Free guided tours run in spring and summer and an Interpretation Centre is situated at the Leigh Woods end of the bridge.

If you have time walk or cycle over the bridge to the Interpretation Centre. It is well worth the views on either side. To reach the Observatory cross back to the Clifton side and take a path on the left just beyond the bridge.

I♥ Bristol because...

it's so close to some great places like Ashton Court and Leigh Woods with loads of old trees, wild garlic and deer.

8 The Observatory

Litfield Place, Clifton, Bristol, BS8 3LT

Houses a camera obscura that provides breathtaking panoramic views.

Containing one of the few UK camera obscuras open to the public, the Observatory offers a unique view over Clifton and the Avon Gorge. It also houses the entrance to a tunnel running underneath Clifton Downs, which leads to a natural cave. The cave looks out over the Avon Gorge and up to the Suspension Bridge.

From the Observatory follow the lovely, tree-lined path along Clifton Down promenade to the junction with Bridge Valley Road. Turn right here and walk another five minutes until you come to the Zoo on the right-hand side.

(9) Bristol Zoo Gardens

Clifton Down, Bristol, BS8 3HA

Twelve acres of botanical gardens home to 450 animal species.

See case study: 'Sustainable future for wildlife and people' on p. 210.

*There are two bus stops just outside the Zoo going in two directions
towards the city centre and Bristol Temple Meads. If you are cycling you
may like to join the 'Downs and hills' tour at this point or head back into
town via Pembroke Road or Whiteladies Road.*

Victoria Square and Gardens

Directory

 ## Archipeleco

29 Redland Hill, Bristol, BS6 6UX
0117 973 9099
lucy@archipeleco.co.uk
www.archipeleco.co.uk

Architects specialising in sustainable design and consultancy.

 ## Attic Tea

115 Coldharbour Road, Westbury Park, Bristol, BS6 7SD
0117 909 0357
info@attictea.co.uk
www.attictea.co.uk

Award-winning tea house embracing the Chinese tea tradition.

 ## Avon Garden Trust

30 Hurle Crescent, Clifton, Bristol, BS8 2SZ
feedback@parkdetectives.org
www.parkdetectives.org

Educational charity that helps to preserve Bristol's historic parks
and gardens.

 ## Avon Gorge and Downs Wildlife Project

Education Department, Bristol Zoo Gardens, Clifton Down,
Bristol, BS8 3HA
0117 903 0609
mleivers@bristolzoo.org.uk
www.avongorge.org.uk

Events and activities protecting wildlife in this area.

 Avon Wildlife Trust

32 Jacobs Wells Road, Bristol, BS8 1DR
0117 917 7270
mail@avonwildlifetrust.org.uk
www.avonwildlifetrust.org.uk

Works with local people to protect local wildlife.

The Trust is Bristol's leading wildlife charity and an essential resource
for those wanting to learn more about the biodiversity of the area.
Based at the foot of Brandon Hill, it manages nature reserves, carries
out environmental education programmes and hosts several
nature-themed events.

 Bella Deli

17 Chandos Road, Redland, Bristol, BS6 6PG
0117 973 2282

Wholefood store where you bring your own containers.

 Bishop's Knoll

Entrance: Bramble Lane, Bristol, BS9 1RD
01476 581111
wopsmail@woodlandtrust.org.uk
www.woodlandtrust.org.uk

Mature mixed woodland developed naturally over the past 200 years.

 Blue Juice

39 Cotham Hill, Cotham, Bristol, BS6 6JY
0117 973 4800

Café serving wholesome, rejuvenating, tasty soul food.

Born

64 Gloucester Road, Bishopston, Bristol, BS7 8BH
0117 924 5080
enquiries@borndirect.com
www.borndirect.com

Shop helping women make informed choices about pregnancy, childbirth and baby products.

 Boston Tea Party

75 Park Street, Bristol, BS1 5PF
0117 929 3939
bristol@bostonteaparty.co.uk
www.bostonteaparty.co.uk

Popular West Country café using sustainably sourced produce.

 Bristol Community Dance Centre

Bristol Community Dance Centre, Jacobs Wells Road, Hotwells, Bristol, BS8 1DX
0117 929 2118
bristoldance@btconnect.com
www.bristolcommunitydancecentre.co.uk

Offers a large programme of classes for all dance enthusiasts.

The centre is housed in a building that was formerly an Elizabethan theatre, then the John Hipsley Georgian theatre and then a Victorian swimming pool. Today, it hosts classes for a wide range of international dance styles, and is open to all ages and abilities.

 Bristol Kitestore

39a Cotham Hill, Cotham, Bristol, BS6 6JY
0117 974 5010
info@kitestore.co.uk
www.kitestore.co.uk

Sells a wide array of kite-surfing, power and stunt kites.

 Bristol Naturalists' Society

20 Harcourt Hill, Redland, Bristol, BS6 7RB
info@bristolnats.org.uk
www.bristolnats.org.uk

Stimulates a greater awareness of natural history and geology in the Bristol area.

Bristol University Sustainability Team (BUST)

Bristol University Student Union, Queens Road, Bristol, BS8 1LN
0117 954 5800
http://bustbristol.ning.com

Student environmental group promoting awareness about sustainability.

BUST is a student-run group trying to make a difference in and around Bristol University to help create a sustainable future. Its projects include a bicycle surgery and a food cooperative.

Bristol Zoo Gardens

Clifton Down, Bristol, BS8 3HA
0117 974 7300
information@bristolzoo.org.uk
www.bristolzoo.org.uk

Twelve acres of botanical gardens home to 450 animal species.

See case study: 'Sustainable future for wildlife and people' on p. 210.

Cleanup UK

PO Box 2045, Bristol, BS35 1ZL
07796 691220
george.monck@cleanupuk.org.uk
www.cleanupuk.org.uk

National charity that supports volunteer litter groups that keep neighbourhoods clean.

Clifton Arcade

Boyces Avenue, Clifton, Bristol, BS8 4AA
07831 166979
www.cliftonarcade.co.uk

Intimate Victorian shopping arcade housing a variety of local traders.

Clifton Lido

Oakfield Place, Clifton, Bristol, BS8 2BJ
0117 933 9530
spa@lidobristol.com
www.lidobristol.com

Restored Victorian lido with restaurant, spa, swimming pool and poolside bar.

Clifton Suspension Bridge Trust

Bridge Road, Leigh Woods, Bristol, BS8 3PA
0117 974 4664
bridgemaster@cliftonbridge.org.uk
www.cliftonbridge.org.uk

Information centre and dramatic views of the Avon Gorge.

 # Cotham Gardens

Off Redland Grove, Redland, Bristol, BS6
www.rcas.org.uk

Lovely, intimate park in the heart of a leafy residential neighbourhood.

 # Cotham Hill Bakery

8 Cotham Hill, Bristol, BS6 6LF
0117 973 0339

Much-loved family bakery using locally sourced ingredients.

North Central fact :

An incredible 97% of respondents in Stoke Bishop feel that they have been in fine fettle during the past year.

 # The Downs

Off Stoke Road, Clifton, Bristol, BS9
0117 922 3719
bristolparks@bristol.gov.uk

Very popular open parkland between Clifton and Westbury Park.

 # Friends of Brandon Hill

Entrance: off Jacobs Wells Road, Bristol, BS1
info@friendsofbrandonhill.org

Community group supporting the management of this ancient park.

Friends of Old Sneed Park Nature Reserve

Entrance: south-east corner of Glenavon Park, Stoke Bishop, Bristol, BS9 1RN
fospnrjar@yahoo.co.uk
http://spnaturereserve.com

Voluntary group that runs this beautiful council-owned nature reserve.

Friends of St Andrews Park

St Andrews Park, Effingham Road, St Andrews, Bristol, BS6 5BA
http://friendsofstandrewspark.ning.com

Maintain the park as a cherished asset for the local community.

Gales of Westbury Park Butchers and Gamedealers

31 North View, Westbury Park, Bristol, BS6 7TT
0117 973 6177

Sells meat from the family farm, wild game and homemade pies.

Hotwells and Cliftonwood Community Association

3 Charles Place, Hotwells, Bristol, BS8 4QW
0117 929 1883
admin@hotwellscliftonwood.org.uk
www.hotwellscliftonwood.org.uk

Charitable organisation working for the local community.

This neighbourhood association has existed for more than 30 years. It works to enable people in the area to have greater control over decision-making processes that affect their lives, to tackle social, political and environmental problems in the neighbourhood, and to help develop a sustainable local economy.

The Hub at Bristol University

Bristol University Student Union, Queen's Road, Bristol, BS8 1LN
0117 954 5800
www.ubu.org.uk

Network of social, environmental and development societies connecting students with causes.

Kitchen Garden Group, Hotwells Primary School

Hotwells Primary School, Hope Chapel Hill, Hotwells, Bristol, BS8 4ND
0117 903 0044

Small kitchen garden in which pupils grow fruit and vegetables.

Since 2005, the school has kept a small kitchen garden within the grounds, cultivated by the children. The fresh produce is sometimes incorporated into school lunches. Known as the Garden for Life, the patch is managed mainly by a committed group of parent volunteers.

Leigh Court Farm

Pill Road, Abbots Leigh, Bristol, BS8 3RA
01275 375756
mail@leighcourtfarm.org.uk
www.leighcourtfarm.org.uk

Grows organic fruit and vegetables for a box scheme and farmers markets.

See case study: 'Food for the city in Bristol's hinterland' on p. 211.

Metford Road Community Orchard

1 Metford Road, Redland, Bristol, BS6 7LA
karen.shergold@virgin.net

Thriving orchard run by volunteers from around Redland.

modoto

Chandos House, 128 Cotham Brow, Bristol, BS6 6AE
0117 230 0128
liz.zeidler@modoto.co.uk
www.modoto.co.uk

Consultancy that supports leadership change and community empowerment.

This Bristol-based consultancy offers leadership courses and one-to-one coaching to support individuals and organisations trying to turn their visions into reality. In particular, it works with people attempting to bring about change to build a more sustainable world. modoto helps its clients to overcome challenges and develop strong, positive teamwork.

Nest Building

59 Redland Road, Bristol, BS6 6AQ
0117 911 4528
info@nestbuilding.co.uk
www.nestbuilding.co.uk

Ecological builders and consultancy specialising in making homes more energy efficient.

 ## The Observatory

Litfield Place, Clifton, Bristol, BS8 3LT
0117 974 1242

Houses a camera obscura that provides breathtaking panoramic views.

 ## Orpheus Cinema

Northumbria Drive, Henleaze, Bristol, BS9 4HN
08712 303200
www.scottcinemas.co.uk

1930s cinema showing a film programme for all ages.

 ## Oxfam Books and Music

1 Queens Road, Bristol, BS8 1QE
0117 929 4890
oxfamshopf2811@oxfam.org.uk

Wide range of books and music, and ethically sourced food and gifts.

 ## Recession

8 Jacobs Wells Road, Bristol, BS8 1EA
www.recessionshop.webs.com

Second-hand clothes shop with some vintage gems.

See case study: 'A new lease of life' on p. 212.

Redland Park United Reform Church

Whiteladies Road, Bristol, BS6 6SA
0117 330 9910
www.redlandparkchurch.co.uk

Church with 48 solar panels on its roof, generating 8 kWh.

 # Scoopaway

113 Gloucester Road, Bristol, BS7 8AT
0117 987 2199
info@scoopawayhealthfoods.co.uk

Sells organic, vegetarian and wholefood produce by the scoopful.

 # Sustainable Energy Installations

St Brandon's House, 29 Great George Street, Bristol, BS1 5QT
0117 214 0610
www.sei-energy.co.uk

Designs, supplies and installs renewable energy solutions.

 # Sustainable Redland

26 Broadway Road, Bristol, BS7 8ES
01278 793186
hamishwills@btinternet.com
www.sustainableredland.org.uk

Neighbourhood organisation promoting a low-energy lifestyle.

See case study: 'Supporting each other to take action' on p. 213.

 # Triodos Bank

11 The Promenade, Bristol, BS8 3NN
0117 973 9339
www.triodos.co.uk

Ethical bank for savers who want to support sustainable investment.

Originating in the Netherlands, the Bristol branch of Triodos is very supportive of the local area and committed to sustainable banking. The bank only invests in and lends to organisations that benefit people and the environment.

Whiteladies Road Farmers and Fairtrading Market

Junction of Apsley Road and Whiteladies Road, Bristol, BS8 2RL

http://sustainableredland.org.uk

Set up by Sustainable Redland, operating two Saturdays a month.

Wind Prospect

7 Berkeley Square, Clifton, Bristol, BS8 1HG

0117 301 7151

info@windprospect.com

www.windprospect.com

Global renewable energy business with offices worldwide.

Wind Prospects began in Bristol and is now one of the most successful independent renewable energy developers in the world. The company is an inspiring example of how green technologies can be both commercially viable and reduce our reliance on fossil fuels.

Bristol Zoo Gardens

Sustainable future for wildlife and people

More than 450 animal species are housed at Bristol Zoo Gardens, a beautifully landscaped 12-acre site in the heart of Clifton. One of Bristol's biggest tourist attractions, the zoo celebrates its 175th anniversary in 2011. It is using this landmark to do more than just look back at its past: it has big plans for the future too. These include expanding projects in the conservation of biodiversity and environmental sustainability. The zoo's work goes far beyond simply providing families with a good day out.

On site, the zoo has a strategic approach to sustainability, taking into account water usage, carbon, waste management, procurement, transport, travel and biodiversity. Director Dr Jo Gipps believes that environmentalism should be at the heart of any enterprise, not just tacked on as a token effort. The zoo has more than 350 volunteers and outreach programmes in the community that inform the public on how to adopt sustainable and wildlife-friendly lifestyles.

Through the Bristol Conservation and Science Foundation the zoo also carries out extensive conservation work in the field, both in the UK and abroad. With projects across South America, Africa and Asia the Foundation uses its expertise to tackle conservation problems and to aid communities facing environmental challenges. Its activities include protecting penguins in South Africa from oiling and working with the Asian Turtle Network in Vietnam to protect several species threatened with extinction. Closer to home, the Foundation helps conserve the rare plants and animals that inhabit the Avon Gorge.

There are further grand plans for the future of Bristol Zoo. Planning permission was recently approved for the National Wildlife Conservation Park, which will be spread over a 55-hectare site near Cribbs Causeway and will be the first conservation-led animal visitor attraction in the UK. The project will link specific ecosystems and conservation projects across the world with exhibits at the park that will house a wide range of wild animals. The ecosystems will include the Congolese tropical rainforests and an Indian Ocean coral reef.

Leigh Court Farm

Food for the city in Bristol's hinterland

Organic fruit and vegetables grow in abundance at Leigh Court, a farm based on the Leigh Court estate just outside Bristol. It supplies the city with one of the most local fruit and veg box schemes available and sells produce at weekly farmers markets, including those in Corn Street and Whiteladies Road, and at the monthly village market in Abbots Leigh. There is also a farm shop at Leigh Court. The farm is employee-owned and has four staff taking on different roles. Chris Loughlin, a market gardener from Pennsylvania, has been the manager since 1999 and has expanded the farm from three to 25 acres.

Leigh Court is unusual in that it exists on entirely rented land. 'This is the future of local production,' says Chris, 'otherwise it will remain in the domain of the very rich. You can't buy farmland these days and expect a return from what you've spent on it.' Production is spread over four fields within a five-mile radius: the walled garden in Abbots Leigh, Portbury field, Failand Front Ground and part of Bathing Pool fields in Wraxall. The varied soil types and microclimates on these different sites enable the farm to grow a wide range of crops.

The walled garden in Abbots Leigh is a warm, protected and picturesque spot. It was built by the Victorian owners to grow exotic food to impress their guests: producing just one pineapple here would have cost the equivalent of £1,000. Today the garden has ideal growing conditions with high walls, a shelter belt of mature trees and soil that was nourished by the Victorians' horse manure sweepings. It produces French beans, runner beans, courgettes, cherries, pears, plums, apples and apricots. Polytunnels increase the yield with tomatoes, cucumbers and basil. The more acidic soil at Portbury is good for potatoes, brassicas and root crops, and, at Failand, cabbages, calabrese and squash.

The farm has now reached its optimum size. 'It's time to intensify not extensify production by introducing Spanish style polytunnels,' Chris declares. These will produce a few delicious surprises for the boxes in the 'hungry gap' of early spring.

Recession

A new lease of life

Have you ever been amazed at all the clothes your family and friends have at home gathering dust and thought, 'they could run a shop with this'. This is what occurred to Gill Loats in 2008 and led her to set up her business Recession — a second-hand shop for clothes that have a story to tell.

'It was a great time to launch the shop. People were searching for an individual look and vintage is good for that,' says Gill, who finds that the clothes just keep on coming. 'People like to know there is a use for things they no longer want.' Her clients like the idea of buying in a shop that recycles and they love her chic, reasonably priced outfits, which allow them to discover their own style.

With its green celery mannequin at the door, and its cornucopia of vintage treasures inside, Recession has become quite a tourist attraction. Located at the bottom of Jacobs Wells Road, it's just five minutes walk from the harbour and the city centre.

In April 2010, Gill ran a fashion show at the Southbank Club in Bedminster using clothes from her shop. It was such a success that she ran another one six months later. Gill has also been the director for the Hotwells and Southville pantomimes, and has lent clothes to the City of Bristol College for their drama courses. Her dream is to open a bigger shop some day and run seasonal fashion shows and performances. She hopes that more people will develop unusual, creative businesses that, like hers, will save rather than use as many resources as possible.

Sustainable Redland

Supporting each other to take action

Sustainable Redland (Susred) has been running since March 2005, largely due to Hamish Wills. Walking down the street one day he found himself blaming a long list of people for inaction on climate change, then realised he hadn't included himself. So he wrote a letter asking people in his neighbourhood to join him in finding ways to adopt a less energy-intensive lifestyle. He delivered 600 letters and received 20 responses: of these, 13 people arrived at the first meeting and Sustainable Redland was born.

The group decided to focus on sustainability and carbon emissions in terms of food, waste and recycling, transport and domestic energy. Realising they had much to learn about these issues they launched bi-monthly meetings with specialist speakers. Out of these meetings came the idea for the Whiteladies Road Farmers Market, one of Susred's first initiatives. It was set up to provide local residents with the opportunity to purchase high-quality, locally grown food and to raise awareness about food miles. The market has always run fortnightly but in 2010 funding was secured to employ a marketing expert with the aim of doubling footfall and running the market weekly.

Other Susred projects and public events include obtaining price reductions on solar panel installations for members, public debates with councillors and local MPs, setting up a gardening club and visiting local edible gardens. The group also runs an effective website and newsgroup that provides information sources and a platform for discussion. It collaborates with other local groups, such as those in the Transition movement, the Redland and Cotham Amenities Society, the local Neighbourhood Partnership, Metford Community Orchard and the Community Farm set up just outside Bristol in Chew Magna.

Sustainable Redland is a well established neighbourhood organisation and it encourages people to get involved either by becoming a member or by buying as much local food as possible, leaving their cars behind, and pooling resources to reduce their carbon footprint. Through its activities the group sends a clear message that a low-energy lifestyle is not only beneficial to our environment, it's healthier, less stressful and more fun.

St Pauls Carnival

Festivals

Spring

March
Bristol Beer Festival

April
Bristol Art Fringe (Montpelier), Eastside Roots Fair, Montpelier Arts Trail, Spike Island Open Studios (April/May), Studio Upstairs Open Studios (April/May)

May
Mayfest (theatre), Bristol Vegan Fayre, Bristol Green, Ethical Food and Music Festival, Bristol Eco Veggie Fair, Montpelier Bean Feast, CrimeFest, Redland May Fair, Southbank Bristol Arts Trail, Dot to Dot Music Festival, Stokes Croft Festival, Bristol Festival of Photography (May/June), Venn Festival (May/June)

Summer

June
St Werburghs Farm Summer Fayre, Easton Arts Trail, Jamaica Street Artists Open Studios, Festival of Nature, Stokes Croft Street Fest, Bristol Design Festival, Bristol's Biggest Bike Ride, Bristol National Refugee Week, Redfest (Redfield) (June/July)

July
St Pauls Carnival, Boogie for Brizzle at Bristol Zoo, Shakespeare Festival (open air), St Mark's Road Street Party, Oxjam (July/August), Bristol Harbourside Festival (July/August)

August
Old Duke Jazz Festival, Bristol Cider Festival, Bristol International Balloon Fiesta, Pride Day

Balloon Fiesta

Autumn

September
Bristol International Kite Festival, Bristol Festival, Organic Food Festival, Bristol Doors Open Day, Bristol Green Doors, Youth4Youth Festival (Kingswood), Bristol Poetry Festival, BrisFest, St Werburghs Art Trail, Best of Bedminster Show (September/October)

October
West Bristol Arts Trail, Art on the Hill (Windmill Hill), Mivart Street Open Studios, Harmonica Festival (Folk House), Cajun and Zydeco Festival, Boiling Wells Apple Day and Wassailing (October/November), Wildscreen Festival (every other October)

November
North Bristol Arts Trail, Front Room (Totterdown Arts Trail), Encounters International Film Festival

Winter

December
Picton Street Festive Fayre, Hartcliffe Christmas Fairy Lights

January
Silent Comedy Festival, Bristol Storytelling Festival (January/February)

Across the year

Festival of Ideas, You and Your Work, Love Food Festivals

Afterword

by Peter Madden

Throughout its history, Bristol has been an important and influential place. In mediaeval times the thriving port made it England's second city. As global trade expanded, its merchants and adventurers carried the name of Bristol to the furthest corners of the globe. By the time of the industrial revolution—and Brunel's innovations—it was famous as a centre for manufacturing and engineering.

Now, in the early decades of the 21st century, it is time for Bristol to reinvent itself again. I believe it can do this by becoming a world-leading sustainable city. This would help to secure our future prosperity and ensure that Bristol remains a fantastic place in which to live.

Environmental issues will inevitably play a huge role in the planet's future. On current trends, the world population will reach more than nine billion by 2050. And all these billions will no doubt aspire to have comfortable, affluent lifestyles. But there are limits to what the planet can provide. We will see shortages of land to feed ourselves, of water to drink, of oil to run our economies. And we will face the inevitable consequences of pollution and climate change. The cities that will prosper in the 21st century are those that invest now in a shift to a low carbon economy and start to build their resilience against the coming storms.

As this guide shows, Bristol is well-placed to become one of the most sustainable cities of our time. It is home to some highly influential green organisations and it has developed a vibrant and growing environmental technologies sector, with cutting edge 'green tech' businesses and universities. Many Bristolians are growing their own food or buying from local producers. And the council is starting to tackle the city's environmental impact, with many recycling programmes and ambitious plans to reduce carbon dioxide emissions.

This is an impressive start, but there is a long way to go. While Bristol makes a strong claim to be the UK's 'green capital', it falls far short of what is being achieved in the most sustainable cities elsewhere in Europe. There is much for us to do in the decades to come.

Bristol Harbourside

As any Bristolian knows, transport in the city still leaves a lot to be desired. Our housing and buildings, while often picturesque, leak energy. Many people in our poorer communities face a depressing environment outside their front doors. And if everyone in the world had the same lifestyle and used the same quantity of resources as the average Bristolian, the global population would need three planet Earths to sustain it.

So, we cannot be complacent. It is going to need each of us, as citizens of Bristol, to do our bit. As this guide shows, there are a huge number of initiatives across the city in which to get involved—including my organisation, Forum for the Future. So there is no excuse! We must also encourage local government and businesses to play their part and show some real leadership.

Like those sailors of yore setting out to find new lands, Bristol must now embark on a new voyage of discovery to find different ways to live and alternative sources of prosperity. And as we make that voyage, every one of us must crew and steer the ship.

Peter Madden lives in Bristol and is Chief Executive of Forum for the Future, the independent sustainability experts.

St Werburghs Fayre

Acknowledgements

Many people and organisations assisted with the preparation of this guide. We would like to thank the excellent team that has used its combined talents to produce the book, and our generous sponsors. In particular:

Researchers:

Helène Deniaud, Louisa Dennison, Lucy Fleetwood (main researcher), Hannah James, Ben Melarickas and Massimo Torsello.

Writers:

Emmelie Brownlee, Sarah Flint, Clare Groom, Kirsty Matthewson, Kesty Morrison, Emilie Rowell, Hayley Thompson and Eleanor Williamson—all Ecojam writers; and Lucy Fleetwood, James Hairsnape, Ruth Hendry, Gonzalo Fernando Marcos, Kate Sykes, Lucille Smith and Clare Wilks.

At Alastair Sawday Publishing:

Tom Dixon, Chris Elmes, Jackie King, Rob Richardson, Alastair Sawday (as publisher and Chair of the Bristol Green Capital Initiative), Toby Sawday and Annie Shillito.

At Bristol Green Capital Initiative:

Dan Green (as Vice Chair), Mark Leach (as Co-ordinator), Steve Marriott, Alex Minshull and Daniel Oliver.

Sponsors:

Bristol City Council (as main sponsor); Bristol Zoo Gardens with Bristol Natural History Consortium, along with Forum for the Future, Garrad Hassan, GWE Business West, The Converging World and Westmark Developments (as joint sponsors); Bevan Brittan, Gregg Latcham Solicitors and Bart Spices (as financial contributors).

The Monkey Jungle at Bristol Zoo

Others who have given valuable time and information:

Ben Barker, Greater Bedminster Partnership; Martin A Bates, Indexer; Alan Boldon, Arts and Ecology Research Group; Bristol City Council Sustainability City Group; Bristol City Council Transport Service; Savita Custead, Bristol Natural History Consortium; George Ferguson, Tobacco Factory; Carolyn Hassan, Knowle West Media Centre; Andrew Kelly, Festival of Ideas; Hamish Mills, Sustainable Redland; Philip Morgan, Proof Reading; Faye Nightingale and Jess Trethowan as our launch co-ordinators; Sam Parker, Neighbourhood Partnership Manager; Paul Rainger, Forum for the Future; Raj Shankari, Love Easton; The Source Magazine; Kristin Sponslor, Transition Bristol; Jane Stephenson, Bristol Friends of the Earth; Sue Walker, Hartcliffe Health and Environment Action Group; Mike and Liz Zeidler, Happy City Initiative and Rachel Fleming and Catharine Stott from The Source Magazine as our distributors.

To the many others who contributed but have not been mentioned here by name, please accept our heartfelt appreciation and gratitude. This book represents the combined effort, learning and achievements of hundreds of people from across Bristol. Thank you for sharing your information and stories to enable this guide to come about.

The Downs

Photo credits

Wind turbines at Avonmouth

Index